Preface

In some ways, the main idea for this book has been gestating for a long time. In my classes and writings, I have always tried to emphasize the extent to which law is not so much a science or even an intellectual system. Instead, I have played up the rich historical context in which law arises and functions; it is a dynamic mix of personalities, circumstances, and politics. However, the more immediate impetus to write about the common law and its great cases in a way that was directed primarily to nonlawyers came in 2008. I was invited by Holland-America to give a series of talks on a leg of one of its world cruises. I decided that it would be an excellent opportunity to try out my ideas. Even if I say so myself, it turned out to be a great success: people seemed to be genuinely fascinated by these tales and thought it a wonderful way to access the other-wise dense and unfriendly world of legal scholarship. I am grateful to Carolyn Craig for her invitation to give the lectures and to all the guests who found it worthwhile to forgo the more obvious pleasures of sun and sea to attend my talks.

In researching and writing this book, I have relied extensively on the fine body of research that has developed over the years on all these great cases. I have done little original or primary research myself. With full acknowledgment of gratitude, I have been as comprehensive as possible in listing those sources at the end of the book. Also, although I have not followed the old adage "not to let the facts get in the way of a good story," I have taken the liberty of selecting the most fascinating or plausible interpretation of the available historical evidence where there is uncertainty or doubt.

As usual, many people have played important parts in helping me complete this book. I have benefited from a host of critics and colleagues, mostly friendly, who have shared their time and insights. In particular, I am grateful to Bruce Mann, Derek Morgan, Beverly Myhal, Marilyn Pilkington, Bruce Ryder, Joe Singer, Mark Tushnet, and Kevin Washburn, for reading earlier drafts of chapters and for preventing me from making even more startling errors and omissions. However, my greatest debt is to my two research assistants, Cynthia Hill and Tiffany Herbert-Ramsubick, who did a simply splendid job in bringing together all the available sources and research; they made writing this book both the easiest and the most enjoyable of tasks. And, to Ian Langlois for putting the book to bed with his characteristic rigor and insight, *many thanks*.

Allan C. Hutchinson
February 2010

1

In Praise of Great Cases

The Big, the Bad, and the Goodly

For many, the law appears as an impenetrable thicket of rules and principles. Its origins are considered murky, its personnel are viewed with an odd mix of suspicion and respect, and its application to particular situations seems elusive at best. Much of this popular bemusement is warranted. Lawyers take little effort to make the law as open or available as it could be. Indeed, some lawyers seem intent on making the law as inaccessible and obtuse as it can be. It is not surprising, therefore, that, on encountering the law or trying to appreciate its complexity, many will share Alfred Lord Tennyson's frustration at what appears to be "the lawless science of our law – That codeless myriad of precedent, That wilderness of single instances." It is an uninviting edifice for the curious citizen.

It is true that understanding the law can be a daunting prospect. Yet behind its professional and often-inscrutable facade, there is much about the law that is as exciting and as stirring as any other area of human endeavor. After all, at its most basic, law is little more than a site at which one group of people attempt to resolve the problems and disputes of others. Although framed in all sorts of off-putting language and occurring in impersonal institutional settings, the legal process is really a rich slice of social life. It offers an illuminating look at one of the more important ways in which society functions. This is especially so about the so-called common law and its great cases.

In concentrating on some of the law's great cases, this book is not about the big law cases that are so often in the media spotlight – O. J. Simpson, Paul Bernardo, and the like. Even though people's lives are so affected by the law, there is a dearth of knowledge of how it comes to be and how it operates. This book is about shedding some light on the actual cases that lawyers consult and that law students are required to study. In that sense, it offers a rare glimpse into the seemingly opaque world of lawyers and law students.

By looking at the common law's great cases, I hope to avoid presenting the law as a foreign country in which its residents speak a convoluted jargon, engage in mysterious rituals, and add small print to all their communications. Instead, I want to show the law as the living, breathing, and down-the-street experience that it really is. We can all vacation there and come back refreshed and invigorated.

I will look at the ordinary people whose stories have influenced and shaped the law as well as the characters and institutions (lawyers, judges, and courts) that did much of the heavy lifting.

But before I introduce you to the eight cases that I have chosen, I need to introduce you more generally to the common law and what I mean by "great cases." This is intended to set the context for a better appreciation of these cases and their significance. By understanding what the common law is, it will be easier to grasp why great cases are of such importance. Many of these great cases reach back into the nineteenth century and are drawn from across the globe. But they still hold great sway in the legal world by virtue of their role as the bedrock of legal thinking.

The common law is often taken to refer to the vast body of judicial decisions that has developed over time; judges decide present disputes by reference to past decisions and establish rules for future controversies. Dating back to England in the eleventh century, *common law* originally referred to the customary rules that were adopted by itinerant judges as they sought to develop a 'common' law for the resolution of disputes throughout the country. These judicial episodes do not so much offer focused interpretations of the law or illustrative applications of the law – they are the law; the reasons given by judges for their decisions amount to the law itself. In this sense, although judicial decisions are now reported extensively, the common law is often thought of as unwritten law. It is not collected or contained in any one authoritative code.

Apart from the more formal resources of law, the law is energized by reliance on customary and communal norms of behavior. Law is not only a top-down enterprise: it is also very much a bottom-up exercise. Although traditional sources of law are no longer so prominent as they once were, there are vast tracts of the law that have arisen organically from mercantile or administrative practices (e.g., *caveat emptor*). They developed independently of the courts in their force and effect; it was only later that they received official recognition from judges in later disputes. Customs were accepted as having legal authority if they were continuous, certain, reasonable, and followed. As such, the common law method is the crystallization of such a process and disposition.

Common law can best be appreciated in contrast to legislation. Legislation is an enactment by Parliament, a provincial or state legislature, or a city hall. Whether framed as statutes or contained in delegated regulations, these instruments stipulate certain rules and principles that must be interpreted and followed by the courts. Under the doctrine of legislative supremacy, legislation is superior to the common law. In any conflict between legislation and the common law, legislation will prevail. However, the common law has a historical pedigree that means that judge-made law forms the detailed backdrop against which the enactment and the interpretation of legislation take place.

The depiction of the common law as a practice of lawmaking is as important as the body of legal decisions it produces. The common law is best understood as being an intellectual mind-set to lawmaking as much as a technical practice; lawyers have transformed a natural tendency to use past performance as a guide to future conduct into an institutional imperative. By way of the doctrine of *stare decisis* (to stand by decisions), the common law method insists that past decisions are not only to be considered by future decision makers but also are supposed to be followed and treated as binding. This way of proceeding is defended as providing citizens with a necessary check against the exercise of arbitrary judicial authority in deciding cases.

The traditional virtues of precedential authority (i.e., it produces certainty, allows reliance, curbs arbitrariness, effects equality, and encourages efficiency) are not to be underestimated. But that resort to the legal past need not be restricted to particular decisions made or a mechanical application of them. Judges are considered to judge best when they distill the principled spirit of the past and rely on it to develop the law in response to future new demands. As Lord Leslie Scarman, a high-ranking English judge in the late twentieth century, put it, "Whatever the court decides to do, it starts from a baseline of existing principle and seeks a solution consistent with or analogous to a principle or principles already recognized."

However, like most matters, things are not always what they appear to be; the theory of what is supposed or said to happen is not always congruent with what actually does happen. The challenge for the courts in a rapidly changing world has been to operate the system of precedent wisely so that the need for stability is balanced against the demand for progress: the courts must not allow formal certainty to eclipse substantive justice. The judges have a huge capacity to develop and apply the law in creative ways – they are not the automatons of popular myth. There are a variety of technical tools at their disposal for avoiding or distinguishing precedents. Accordingly, although operating within an official culture of institutional conservatism, all judges and jurists not only acknowledge that the law indeed responds and changes to new circumstances and fresh challenges, but they also celebrate and champion the law's capacity to do so.

One way to understand this common law process is to imagine the existing body of legal decisions as the product of a continuing and sprawling chain-novel exercise. Judges approach the task of giving reasons for judgment in particular cases as if they had been asked to read the many chapters of earlier judgments that have already been written and to contribute a chapter of their own that in some significant way continues the narrative of the common law. Although this process places judges under certain constraints, it also leaves them, like the creative writer, with considerable leeway to interpret what has gone before and to add a few twists and turns of their own. As such, common law is to be found in the unfolding struggle between the openings of adjudicative freedom and the closings of precedential constraint.

In this way, the common law tradition can be grasped as being as much a human process as anything else – it is something that lawyers do as much as what is produced as a consequence of their doing it. The common law is a dynamic and engaged activity in which how judges deal with rules is considered as vital as the resulting content of the rules and actual decisions made. Consequently, the common law is largely characterized by the craft-skills that judges bring to their task; they are social artisans of the first order. This is not to reduce common lawyering or judging to a purely technical proficiency, because the best craftspeople are those who bring vision and imagination as well as technique and rigor to the fulfillment of their discipline. What judges make is as important as how they make it.

So, rather than see the common law as a fixed body of rules and regulations, it is preferable to view it as a living tradition of dispute resolution. Because law is a social practice and society is in a constant state of agitated movement, law is always an organic and hands-on practice that is never the complete or finished article; it is always situated inside and within, not outside and beyond, the society in which it arises. In short, the common law is a *work–in–progress* – evanescent, dynamic, messy, productive, tantalizing, and bottom-up. The common law is always moving but never arriving, is always on the road to somewhere but never getting anywhere in particular, and is rarely more than the sum of its parts and often much less.

There is no better symbol of the common law's evolutionary quandary than the role of so-called great cases. These are cases that are regarded by almost all lawyers as beacons of the common law tradition. Although their precise import and reach are continuously contested, any credible version of the common law has to be informed and organized around such decisions. Any account of the common law is incomplete and unpersuasive without them. Great cases are generally considered to represent the impressive pragmatic strength of the common law in being able to adapt to fresh challenges and new conditions. They confirm that the common law is much closer to being a political, unruly, and open-ended process than many are prepared to admit.

What counts as a great case is simply whatever people agree to designate as a great case. Of course, although some people, like appellate judges, exercise more clout than others in this process, court decisions do not attain greatness unless they can attract a critical mass of support among the legal community at large. There is nothing so self-evidently or intrinsically great about particular cases that automatically guarantees their inclusion in any jurisprudential hall of fame. At another time and in a different context, great cases might become simply run-of-the-mill affairs or, more usually and more revealingly, monuments to what the law ought not to be or could have been (e.g., segregation, cruelty). This status is as much a matter of communal acceptance as conformity with any universal measure about the virtues of greatness. Or, to put it another way, the quality of greatness is part of this debate rather than an external restraint on it.

That having been said, there does seem to be a general consensus among lawyers on the notion that great cases are those that have become sufficiently and widely accepted over time as to claim central importance in the legal canon. Not only must any future development of the law be able to incorporate the holdings of great cases, but such holdings are treated as capable of pointing in the direction or illu- minating the path that such new development must take. This idea of great cases as "landmarks upon the trackless wilds of the law" or as "fixed stars in the jurisprudential fir- mament" gives a sense of the belief in them as intellectual compasses for legal travelers who are uncertain where to turn or go. However, there is a tendency to treat these great cases as more enduring and certain than they actually are; even stars explode or implode over time, and their fixity is always relative to location. There is nothing natural or given about their status: their identification is more a process of discovery than creation. Great cases stand both as markers for wayward or lost lawyers and as reminders of the legal community's collective faith in the common law tradition and method.

Rather than view great cases as fixed stars or landmarks, I think that it is more appropriate to think of them as temporary lighthouses, designed with a particular purpose in mind, constructed with available materials, and with a limited working life. As society moves, the need for such constructions fades and other, more useful devices are designed to take their place. As with celebrity, greatness in law is no less dependent on passing trends and shifting contexts. Once the values that underpin a case no longer garner sufficient support or the informing context has changed substantially, a great case will fall by the wayside and be consigned to the rubbish tip of errors, mistakes, and anomalies. Depending on the audience, today's star is yesterday's wannabe or tomorrow's has-been.

Although the stylistic or literary quality of a judgment helps establish its stature as a great case, it is in no way decisive in itself. It is the rhetorical success and political acceptability of the decision that will carry the day. The greatness of great cases is less about their formal attributes than it is about their substantive appeal. It is whether the outcome or judgment manages to strike the right chord with its audience that determines its fate and future significance. Great cases have to earn their authority in the salons and chat rooms of legal and popular opinion. And once that opinion begins to shift, the canonical force of such cases will be affected accordingly. Great cases are only as authoritative as the political and moral values that they represent and by whose forbearance they are held in place.

By placing great cases at the heart of the common law, a different understanding of the common law becomes possible. Rather than maintain the projection of law as a dry and formal discipline, it becomes possible to appreciate it as a much more knockabout and seat-of-the-pants performance. Of course, this does not make law any better or worse. As with all human endeavors, the common law offers a microcosm of social life with its usual cast of personalities and characters. It is as flawed as it is functional, it is as appealing as it is off-putting, it is as polished as it is pockmarked, and it is as prejudiced as it is balanced. It would be surprising if it were any different.

As I hope the eight great cases that I have selected will demonstrate, the common law is a messy, episodic, and experimental effort to respond and adapt to the contingent demands that the society brings forward. If there is a method to the common law's madness, it is to be found in the court's diverse and uncoordinated attempts to adapt to changing conditions and shifting demands. As is nature itself, the common law (like all efforts to explain and understand it) is an untidy exercise in human judgment that seeks to make the best of a bad job; it has a certain experimental, catch-as-catch-can, and anything-might-go sense about it. Lawyers, judges, and academics make a rod for their own backs when they present it as anything more than that. The common law is more tentative than teleological, more inventive than orchestrated, more fabricated than formulaic, and more pragmatic than perfected. And great cases are the best testimony to the common law's depiction as an exciting and boisterous work-in-progress.

2

Is Eating People Wrong?

The Law and Lore of the Sea

As does life itself, law has a long and intimate relationship with art and literature. Although it is often assumed that there is one-way traffic from law to literature, there is something of a both-ways street between law and art. Most times, art relies on and follows law as a source of inspiration. Whether it is Charles Dickens's *Bleak House*, Harper Lee's *To Kill A Mockingbird*, or television's *Law and Order* or *Dixon of Dock Green*, art distills and portrays law and its cast of characters in both flattering and demeaning ways. But on some rare and memorable moments, the trade has been reversed – law and life have followed and echoed the styling of art and literature much to the benefit of most concerned.

One name that has made regular appearances in the annals of law and literature is Richard Parker. More often than not, the sea has been the important background for his many exploits and occasional infamy. A Richard Parker was on board the *Francis Speight* when it sank in 1846. On the law's side of the historical tableau, perhaps the most infamous Parker was the eighteenth-century one who was hanged for his decisive part in the Dore mutiny. However, a more telling legal role was played a few decades later by a lowly cabin boy. Although he met with an unfortunate and gruesome end out in the unforgiving Atlantic Ocean, this Richard Parker went on to be part of a cause célèbre that has achieved storied status as one of the defining moments in the rich life of the common law.

Yachting has always been a pastime of the rich. Less a means of transport, it remains a symbolic activity of conspicuous opulence. And John Henry Want was only too aware of this. A tall man who cut a showy figure with his rugged features and extravagant moustache, "Jack" made his fortune in Australia as a successful maritime lawyer who dabbled in a variety of dubious commercial ventures; his political connections proved invaluable in consolidating his wealth. However, uncomfortable with forever being labeled the arriviste, he sought ways to acquire added prestige and improve his standing in society. In 1883, he traveled to England to purchase a suitable vessel and have it sailed back to Sydney, where he could impress his fellow yacht-club members in the waters off the New South Wales harbor.

An Aldous-built, fifty-two-foot, twenty-ton boat constructed in 1867 caught his eye. It was as much a cruiser
as a yacht, but it had won several races a few years earlier.
He purchased the *Mignonette* – a French term for something
that is cute and adorable – for the relatively cheap price of
£400. Delighted with his purchase, the new owner looked
around for a crew to sail her on the long trip back to Australia: Want himself planned to return the way he came, by
more conventional and spacious means.

Hearing of this opportunity, Captain Tom Dudley came
forward. He was short of stature with reddish hair and
beard. A self-made man of thirty, he had earned himself
quite a reputation as a dependable and intrepid mariner; he
brought distinction to his home port of Tollesbury in Essex,
on the southeast coast of England at the mouth of the river
Blackwater. He was a religious man, ran a tight ship, and
insisted that his crew remain dry. His wife, Philippa, was
a local schoolteacher, and Tom was always on the lookout
for ways to improve his financial condition for the benefit
of his wife and three children. Although he did not relish
being away from his family for such a long time, the trip
to Australia offered substantial remuneration and a chance
to check out possible business opportunities on that burgeoning continent. He seemed an ideal choice as captain for
Want and the *Mignonette*'s sixteen-thousand-mile, 120-day
voyage.

Want engaged Dudley on a generous contract. For
£100 on signing up and a further £100 on delivery of the

Mignonette to Sydney, Dudley was to hire and pay a crew, provide all provisions on the trip, and keep her in good repair. It seemed a wonderful deal and one that would leave Dudley with a handsome profit. However, he had problems securing the crew he required. The boat was considered light and small for such an arduous trip through some of the world's most treacherous waters, especially around the Cape of Good Hope. After some initial failures, he recruited a three-man crew of Edwin "Ed" Stephens (as mate), Edmund "Ned" Brooks (as able seaman), and Richard "Dick" Parker (as cabin boy).

The sailing was delayed for a few weeks because the *Mignonette* was in far from shipshape condition. Although many timbers were rotten and needed replacing, the parsimonious Dudley opted to make only minimal and make-do repairs. After extended and agitated negotiations with the Board of Trade over acquiring the necessary documents to certify the ship's seaworthiness, the *Mignonette* and her crew were finally cleared to leave (or, at least, not prevented from leaving). Like most seamen, Dudley was of a superstitious temperament. Although he was ready to sail on a Friday, he chose to wait until the following, less ill-starred Monday. Consequently, the ship set sail for Australia from Southampton on May 19, 1884.

The first weeks were smooth sailing and went off without incident. The crew members were gelling well – the mate, Ed Stephens, a thirty-seven-year old father of five, was a seasoned campaigner who had a few scrapes with shipping authorities a decade or so earlier; the seaman, Ned Brooks, was an old companion of Dudley's and saw the voyage as a cheap way to emigrate to Australia; the cabin boy, Dick Parker, was an orphaned seventeen-year old who hoped that the voyage would make a man of him and open a new life for him. Picking up fresh supplies at Cape Verde on June 8, the *Mignonette* sailed into the windier and rougher seas of the South Atlantic. They avoided the more populated shipping lines to benefit from the strong southeast trade winds and made good time. However, on July 3, the winds fell and, in the proverbial calm before the storm, the ship was briefly becalmed.

The winds soon picked up, and a couple of days later, on July 5, they were in the teeth of a full-scale storm. Dudley ordered his edgy crew to heave to and go below deck. As the ship was now located about 1,600 miles northwest of the Cape of Good Hope and 680 miles from the nearest land on the island of Tristan da Cunha, Dudley's decision to scrimp on repairs no longer seemed like such a good idea. The ship was hit by an enormous wave, and a large hole appeared in the lee bulwarks, some of which had deteriorated further since leaving Southampton. Dudley knew that this was a devastating blow and made the only decision available to him – to abandon ship.

The ship's lifeboat, a flimsy thirteen-foot craft that was more like a dinghy, was lowered and preparations were made to leave the *Mignonette* to its watery fate. Buffeted by the storm and beginning to panic, the four of them were unable

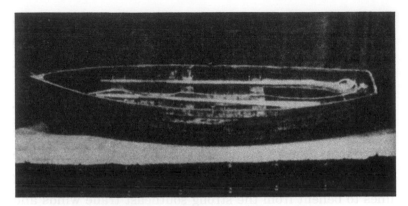

Figure 2.1. The *Mignonette*'s lifeboat on display.

to take much with them by way of equipment or provisions into the lifeboat. A cask of water and some tins of food were lost to the crashing waves. As they pushed off and left the sinking *Mignonette* to its final five minutes of existence, they had managed to salvage only two tins of food, one by Dudley and the other by Parker; they had no drinking water at all. So poorly resourced, their prospects looked very bleak. No one, not least themselves, would have given them much chance of surviving long in their makeshift vessel and off normal trade routes.

The first night, the foursome had to fight off the attentions of a persistent shark. But this was only the first of their ordeals. Aside from having only two cans of turnips and no water, they had no shelter from the elements and no implements with which to fish. After a day or so, the storm subsided and they gratefully shared one can of the turnips. A couple of days later, they managed to haul on board a sleeping turtle whose meat, along with the remaining tin of turnips, offered respite for a little longer. A week into their ordeal, they were much the worse for wear and began drinking their own urine. With little help in sight, or even likely, they began to explore any options available to them.

Since at least the times of the Greeks, it had apparently been maritime tradition that, in such desperate circumstances as the *Mignonette*'s crew found themselves, a cannibalistic solution might be mooted. The theory was that it was better that a couple of men sacrificed themselves in order that the remainder might survive. First, the blood would be drunk and then the flesh consumed; the bodily extremities, like the head, were to be spared and buried at sea. Although the bodies of those who died would be used first, the preferred method of selection was by drawing lots. However, manipulation was often practiced and the alleged number of higher-ranked crew who avoided pulling the short straw was far greater than any normal statistical pattern would expect. Although Dudley was willing to move ahead with such a plan, Stephens and Brooks thought that it was still too premature for such a drastic measure.

After another few days and over two weeks of drifting in the lifeboat, Parker became seriously ill. He had likely been drinking seawater at night and the resulting diarrhea was simply worsening the parlous condition of his already-dehydrated body. He became delirious and was drifting in and out of consciousness. It had been eight days since they had eaten anything, and Stephens was also beginning to deteriorate quickly. Dudley again raised the possibility of drawing lots. Stephens was better disposed to this possibility, but Brooks wanted no part of the macabre scheme. Parker was barely hanging on and in no condition to contribute to their sparse and sporadic exchanges.

On the nineteenth day of their ordeal, Dudley announced that, if no vessel appeared by the next day, then they should kill Parker. As he was already on death's door, Dudley considered that such a course of action was entirely warranted. With no vessel in sight, Dudley assumed responsibility for killing Parker or, as he preferred to think of it, simply accelerating his death by a day or so in order that the other three of them might have a better chance of surviving and being rescued. After all, Dudley maintained that Parker was the obvious choice, as he not only was the weakest and closest to death but also had no wife or children. Stephens reluctantly agreed, but Brooks remained silent at the other end of the boat, neither agreeing nor protesting.

So with a prayer, but with little other ceremony, Dudley slit Parker's throat. Dudley and Stephens were joined by Brooks in drinking Parker's blood: slaking their burning thirst was the first priority. Driven by their hunger, they had little compunction from feeding on his body for the next three days, eating his more digestible inner organs first. But four days after killing Parker and now twenty-four days after abandoning the *Mignonette*, the remaining trio of seafarers began to lose all hope.

Unlike so many other sailors who had simply perished on the open seas, Dudley and his two crew were to get the first and only stroke of luck that they needed. On July 29, their prayers were answered by the arrival of the German freighter, the *Montezuma*, which was on its way from Chile to Hamburg with a cargo of nitrate. Under the command of the solicitous Captain P. H. Somensen, its crew rescued the lifeboat's occupants. Brooks was able to climb on board himself, but Dudley and Stephens were so weak that they had to be hauled up by rope. Not surprisingly, they were in a pitiable condition with wasted bodies, blackened lips, and swollen limbs. However, in a telling gesture, Dudley did not try to hide what had happened. He insisted that the lifeboat should be brought aboard and the scant remains of Parker, a rib and some flesh, should also be preserved. His plan was to give Parker a decent Christian burial back in England.

It took a good month or so before Dudley, Stephens, and Brooks and Parker's remains made it home to England. They arrived back in Falmouth on September 6, having been picked up a few days earlier by a pilot in the English Channel. From the first moment that they returned, Dudley was open and candid about what had happened; he told Collins, the pilot, that a fourth man had been killed and eaten. Apart from bringing back Parker's remains, they were also entirely forthright in their reports to the authorities.

As required by the Merchant Shipping Act of 1854, they made statements at the local customshouse to the shipping master, a Mr. Cheesman. He was a roguish fellow who was as interested in filling his own pockets by conveniently turning a blind eye to smuggling as fulfilling his more mundane and less profitable official duties. The threesome gave details about the wreck as well as Parker's death. For both Dudley and Stephens, the events were regrettable, but in line with expected standards of maritime conduct in such fraught circumstances: "on the twentieth day the lad Richard Parker was very weak through drinking salt water. [I], with the assistance of Mate Stephens, killed him to sustain the existence of those remaining, they being all agreed the act was absolutely necessary." Dudley related the tale with an enthusiasm and such detail that it verged on the unseemly.

Because the *Mignonette* was a small vessel with no passengers or cargo and no substantial loss of life, Mr. Cheesman showed little interest. With no prospect of receiving any perks himself, he determined that there was little more to do and that matters should rest. His mandate was improving safety, not pursuing criminal sanctions. Cheesman sent his report to the Board of Trade in London. Unsure how to proceed, Board of Trade officials forwarded the file to the Home Office, which had ultimate authority for the administration of the courts and criminal prosecutions. As it was a Friday, no decision was expected until after the weekend, and only by Monday at the earliest.

However, from Dudley and Stephens's point of view, it was at this point that events took an unexpected turn for the worse. Just when they thought that their troubles were coming to an end, the person who many consider the villain of the piece came on the scene. While Dudley and Stephens were being interviewed and giving their statutory depositions to Cheesman, the local police officer, James Laverty, was in attendance. He was a sergeant with the Falmouth Harbour Police Force. In contrast to the delinquent Cheesman, he was a rather sanctimonious Methodist who took a by-the-book approach. Rankled by the customs officer's licentious ways, the sergeant had likely had enough of this official connivance with all manner of petty criminals, like stevedores, prostitutes, thieves, cutpurses, and pirates. Word had spread quickly of the *Mignonette* crew's shipwrecking, and so Laverty had decided to be part of their official debriefing.

Laverty listened intently to Dudley's bold account. When Dudley went into great detail about how he had killed Parker with his knife and actually produced the knife, Laverty asked to take possession of it. Again, confident that he had done nothing wrong and that he was not vulnerable to any criminal action, Dudley handed it over and cautioned Laverty that he wanted to be sure that he got it back as a "souvenir" of their nightmarish experience. This was too much for the officious and ambitious Laverty.

Sergeant Laverty found Dudley to be insufferable in his arrogant recounting of what went on aboard the *Mignonette*'s lifeboat. Rather than wait to see whether Cheesman took further action, Laverty contacted his superiors and sought instructions on whether to bring criminal proceedings against both Dudley and Stephens or either. On his own initiative, Laverty sought to obtain warrants for all three men's arrests on the charge of murder on the high seas. He was first rebuffed by the clerk of the justices, John Genn, who insisted that Laverty obtain the approval of the chair of the local magistrates. This was the mayor of Falmouth, Henry Liddicoat. Although the populist mayor was reluctant to intervene because of the public sentiment on the seamen's side, he felt obliged to at least grant permission to Sergeant Laverty to hold Dudley and Stephens at the police station until their appearance before the magistrates court on the Monday morning. Apparently, the three survivors were being treated to a celebratory dinner by Captain Jose, the superintendent of the sailors' home at which they were staying, when Laverty arrived to arrest them. Dudley in particular was most perturbed at this turn of events but was confident that they would all be released on the Monday and on their way home to the families for a well-earned period of extended convalescence.

The fly in the ointment was that all local magistrates had received strict instructions to defer to the advice of the Treasury Solicitor in all murder cases. Prompted by the clerk of the court, Laverty had, therefore, requested that the men be detained until such guidance was received. A local solicitor, Harry Tilly, was prevailed on to act for the seamen and to seek bail. But the magistrates determined that their hands were tied and that they had no option other than to keep them in custody for a few more days until they received instructions from London.

By Wednesday, the *Mignonette* file had made its way through different levels of bureaucracy at the Home Office. Unclear how to proceed, senior officials had referred the matter directly to the desk of the Home Secretary himself, Sir William Harcourt. By this time, public opinion had begun to voice itself squarely and loudly on the side of the detained men; they had done no wrong and had acted entirely in accord with the tried-and-tested customs of the sea. To depict these embattled men as common criminals rather than as reluctant heroes was considered outrageous. The fact that they had survived such an ordeal was a matter for celebration and condolence, not persecution and prosecution.

Distanced and insulated from such local sentiment, Harcourt was concerned with following the letter of the law. Or, more accurately, he saw this as a convenient occasion to have the letter of the law clarified by a superior court after several failed or lapsed prosecutions on similar facts around the Commonwealth. After consulting with Attorney General Sir Henry James and Solicitor General Sir Farrer Herschel, he gave instructions to the Falmouth magistrates that they should proceed to prosecute.

However, upon the men's appearance on September 11, Tilly had managed to obtain bail for them. Surety was posted by John Burton, the proprietor of the famous Old

Curiosity Shop in Falmouth, in the amounts of £400 for Dudley, £400 for Stephens, and £200 for Brooks. Perhaps most startlingly and in a gesture that reinforced growing public opinion, Daniel Parker, the eldest brother of the unfortunate Richard, appeared in his yachtsman's outfit and made a point of publicly shaking the hands of all three fellow seamen. So inflamed were people that a death threat was made against Mayor Liddicoat and ballads began to be sung about the threesome. Indeed, Dudley sent a letter to the *Times* of London in which he expressed his "thanks for numerous favours of sympathy to myself and companions for our past unparalleled sufferings and privation on the ocean, and our present torture under the ban of the law, being charged with an act which certainly was not accompanied by either premeditation or malice in the true sense of the word, as my conscience can affirm." None of this did anything to change the Home Secretary's stance. If anything, it merely galvanized Sir William Harcourt's determination to settle such matters once and for all.

The prosecution was entrusted to a young junior treasury counsel, William Danckwerts, who went on to become a king's counsel and whose son became an eminent judge. He decided that matters would be only further complicated and compromised by keeping Brooks as a defendant, even though he had also feasted on Parker's body. So he offered no evidence against him at the preliminary hearing, and Brooks was acquitted by the magistrates. Dudley and Stephens, however, were not so fortunate, and they were committed to stand trial in November 1884, at the winter Devon and Cornwall Assizes in Exeter.

From the get-go, the trial was something of a sham; the fix was in. The judge who was scheduled to hear the case, Sir William Robert Grove, was required to step aside. In his place, the Home Secretary installed the more "reliable" Baron Huddleston. A brusque character, Huddleston had a reputation for bullying juries into his way of thinking. Although the son of a seafaring father and with some experience in maritime law, he was no friend to the common sailor. Unsympathetic to the crew's plight and keen to ingratiate himself to his superiors, he made it his task to ensure that Dudley and Stephens were not acquitted.

Still the beneficiaries of strong public support, Dudley and Stephens were represented by Arthur J. H. Collins, Q.C. A leading member of the bar and a local stalwart, this talented and costly lawyer had been paid for by a generous defense fund that had been established by the yachting community. Dudley was at first not inclined to take what he considered "charity" but agreed on the basis that any surplus would be used to create a trust fund for Richard Parker's younger sister. After the jury was impaneled and sworn, the accused pleaded not guilty to murder "by reason of necessity."

The prosecution case was entrusted to Arthur Charles, Q.C. He first laid out his legal case. Although he conceded that the conditions on the lifeboat were dreadful and that the crew faced hopeless odds in trying to survive, he made forceful contentions that there was no necessity defense in English law. Although there had been much academic debate about whether necessity was or should be a defense, Charles was adamant that such a claim had no precedential authority. The necessary requirements of an *actus reus* (guilty act), in that they had taken the life of a living person, and *mens rea* (guilty mind), in that they had taken that life with calculated intentions, were present. A criminal conviction was required, even if clemency might not be unwarranted in such circumstances.

The prosecution's evidence was limited but compelling. A number of people from Falmouth were called to testify, including the relentless Sergeant Laverty, about what had been said and confirmed by Dudley and Stephens on their landing in Falmouth. But the star witness was Ned Brooks. Although a reluctant attester, he gave strong confirmation of what had happened on the lifeboat and recounted the leading role of Dudley and his own refusal to participate in killing Richard Parker. In his cross-examination by defendants' counsel, Collins did not seek to contradict or query this account but contented himself with having Brooks emphasize the dreadful conditions on the lifeboat, Parker's failing health and nearness to death, Brooks's own later cannibalistic feasting on the body, and the apparent hopelessness of their situation.

At the end of the prosecution case and at the beginning of the defense's submissions, Baron Huddleston made a crucial, if damning, intervention. He held that he would not hear any further argument about the defense of necessity. As far as he was concerned, there was no law to support such a defense; this was a matter to be left to an appeal court. So chastised and hampered, Collins had little evidence to offer by way of rebuttal and the trial came to a close.

Baron Huddleston was not finished, however, in making his telling interferences from the bench. Mindful of the strong public sentiment still running in Dudley and Stephens's favor, he took innovative steps to ensure that the jury's hands were tied. Relying on his interpretation of the law, he told the men of the jury that they had two choices – they could find the two accused guilty of murder or they could agree to a "special verdict." With little real choice, the jury returned a special verdict: this meant that they would simply state the facts of the case as they found them and leave it to a higher court to apply the relevant law. Consequently, the jury found that:

> if the men had not fed upon the body of the boy, they would probably not have survived to be picked up and rescued, but would within the four days have died of famine; that the boy, being in a much weaker condition, was likely to have died before them; that at the time of the act in question there was no sail in sight, nor any reasonable prospect of

relief; that under the circumstances there appeared to the one prisoners every probability that, unless they fed, or soon fed, upon the boy or one of themselves, they would die of starvation; that there was no appreciable chance of saving life except by killing someone for the others to eat; that, assuming any necessity to kill anybody, there was no greater necessity for killing the boy than any of the other three men.

On receiving this special verdict, Huddleston renewed the defendants' bail and adjourned the assizes to London's Royal Courts of Justice for November 25. In the intervening days, there was much legal wrangling about the appropriate procedure to be followed. The reconvened assizes was further delayed until December 4, when a surprisingly large bench of five judges assembled as the Divisional Court of the Queen's Bench under the leadership of the Chief Justice, Lord Coleridge, a man of impeccable credentials and genuine power. The relative mild objections by defense counsel Collins to these unusual shenanigans suggested that some kind of deal for Dudley and Stephens was already in place.

The hearing went off with no more surprises or dubious legal maneuvers. Despite pressure from the bench, Collins spent his allotted time canvassing the different legal and ethical arguments that supported the recognition of a defense of necessity – extreme circumstances, the greater good, and a measure of last resort. He called in aid the

American decision of *Holmes* in 1842, which had left open the possibility of necessity in similar shipwrecked conditions. At the conclusion of Collins's submissions, after a short recess, Lord Coleridge announced a unanimous finding that a conviction should be entered with reasons to follow. A shocked Dudley and Stephens were immediately remanded to Holloway Prison to await their sentence.

The court reconvened on Tuesday, December 9, to deliver its reasons and its sentence. Speaking for his colleagues, Lord Coleridge recognized "how terrible their temptation was" and "how awful their suffering." However, he was unswerving in his conclusion that the prisoners had killed a "a weak and unoffending boy" for their own survival at the expense of his; the drawing of lots would have made no difference. Drawing on a rhetorical flourish that would be more at home in the pulpit, Lord Coleridge thundered:

> To preserve one's life is generally speaking, a duty, but it may be the plainest and highest duty to sacrifice it. War is full of instances in which it is a man's duty not to live, but to die.... It is not correct, therefore, to say that there is an absolute and unqualified necessity to preserve one's life.... It is enough in a Christian country to remind ourselves of the Great Example which we profess to follow. It is not needful to point out the awful danger of admitting the principle which had been contended for. Who is to be the judge of this sort of necessity? By what measure is the comparative value of lives to be measured? Is it is be strength, or intellect, or what? It is plain that the principle leaves to

him who is to profit by it to determine the necessity which will justify him in deliberately taking another's life to save his own. In this case the weakest, the youngest, the most unresisting, was chosen. Was it more necessary to kill him than one of the grown men? The answer must be "No."

With the court's reasoning concluded and a conviction for murder confirmed, sentence was passed. To Dudley and Stephens's initial horror, they were sentenced to death by hanging. However, in a sign that all was not as it seemed, the judges did not don the customary black hats in delivering their judgment. In closing, Lord Coleridge made what appeared to be a genuinely heartfelt plea to "the Sovereign to exercise that prerogative of mercy which the Constitution has entrusted to the hands fittest to dispense it." It was the official confirmation that, in securing clarity about the law and ensuring that a defense was not made available that might become "the legal cloak for unbridled passion and atrocious crime," the judicial powers-that-be were willing to keep their side of the bargain.

A couple of days later, on the advice of the Home Secretary, Sir William Harcourt, Queen Victoria exercised mercy and commuted their sentence to six months' imprisonment. Although there were forces in government who pushed for life imprisonment, it was ultimately determined that the lesser and relatively mild sentence would best satisfy the ends of formal justice and appease public opinion.

Bitter and unrepentant, Dudley and Stephens served their sentence and were released from Holloway Prison on May 20, 1885, almost a year to the day that they had left on their fateful voyage on the *Mignonette*.

The defense of necessity to a charge of murder has continued to occupy the attention and intellects of judges, lawyers, and theorists generally. The general response remains that the acknowledgment of such a defense will do more harm than good; it is preferable to treat it more as an excuse that goes to sentencing than a justification that goes to guilt or innocence. The fear remains that it will open up a whole can of worms and people will be running the defense in dubious and ever-broadening situations. As Lord Coleridge warned, it might become "the legal cloak for unbridled passion and atrocious crime." This sentiment has been echoed by other legal luminaries. In 1931, the American judge Benjamin Cardozo insisted that "where two or more are overtaken by a common disaster, there is no right on the part of one to save the lives of some by the killing of another." And in 1979, the English Lord Denning went into moral overdrive when he cautioned that "if hunger were once allowed to be an excuse for stealing, it would open a door through which all kinds of lawlessness and disorder would pass. If homelessness were once admitted as a defence to trespass, no one's house could be safe. Necessity would open a door which no man could shut."

Nonetheless, necessity is not an issue that will go away or lie to rest; its contested popular meaning ensures that. In particular, the focus has been on whether it should be a justification that absolves a person of guilt or whether it should merely excuse the crime by a lesser punishment or penalty. The Supreme Court of Canada has waded into this question on several occasions. Rejecting any mere utilitarian calculus of cost and benefits, it insisted in 1975 that there is no general defense of necessity available to a doctor performing an abortion unless there is strong evidence of dire urgency and an impossibility to comply with the law. However, in a wide-ranging judgment in *Perka* in 1984, Mr. Justice Dickson decided that a narrow defense of necessity was available where its distinguishing feature was "the moral involuntariness of the wrongful action": drug-smugglers who felt compelled to enter Canadian waters to obtain necessary and life-saving repairs for their struggling ship were entitled to plead it as a defense to a charge of smuggling.

In its most recent decision, the Supreme Court took a strong line and confirmed that, though there did exist a defense of necessity, it was extremely limited in scope and availability. A father had intentionally killed his twelve-year-old severely disabled daughter; he claimed that he did this as an act of love so as to spare her from further and unbearable suffering. In upholding the father's conviction, the Court clarified that, to establish necessity, it must be shown that there was imminent peril, lack of reasonable lawful alternatives to actions, and proportionality of harm caused and avoided. However, he was convicted of manslaughter, not murder, and he received a sentence of ten years' imprisonment rather than life. The judges were purposefully vague in reaching any conclusion about whether the defense might be available in Dudley and Stephens's situation, although they did not rule out the possibility.

Although the English courts have for more than a century resisted any temptation to recognize a necessity defense, a crack in their united front appeared in 2000. Conjoined twins were born, but it was soon realized that, if they were not separated, the healthier one as well as the unhealthier one (who had an undeveloped brain and no functioning heart or lungs) would die. As staunch Roman Catholics, the twins' parents refused to give their permission to an operation to separate them, preferring for nature to take its course. On the doctors' application, a High Court judge gave permission for the operation to go ahead despite the parents' strenuous objections. The decision was appealed to the Court of Appeal.

After much soul-searching and emphasizing the "unique circumstances" of the case, the appeal court upheld the judge's decision. The judges began by agreeing with the outcome in Dudley and Stephens's case; there was no rationale for allowing one person to kill another to save their own life. However, they insisted that the situation of the conjoined twins was different – the doctors had no personal gain; the ailing twin was "designated for death"; and the doctors were unable to act in the best interests of both patients. Ironically, the judges relied on a commentary by Sir James Stephens, who stated in the *Digest of the Criminal Law*, published in 1887, shortly after Dudley and Stephens's case:

> An act which would otherwise be a crime may in some cases be excused if the person accused can show that it was done only in order to avoid consequences which could not otherwise be avoided, and which, if they had followed, would have inflicted upon him or others whom he was bound to protect inevitable and irreparable evil, that no more was done than was reasonably necessary for that purpose, and that the evil inflicted by it was not disproportionate to the evil avoided.

Whether this definition is persuasive and whether these conditions had been fulfilled in the case of the conjoined twins are still very much causes for debate and disagreement. Although the Supreme Court of Canada might come to a similar outcome to their English counterparts, it seems equally true that most American courts would not. In negotiating this fraught terrain, the judges have the unenviable task of ensuring that the demands of law and morality, though often complementary but occasionally antagonistic as in these necessity cases, are rendered sufficiently compatible to placate both popular and professional opinion. Whether contemporary judges have made a better job of doing this than Lord Coleridge and his colleagues remains an open question.

Richard Parker's tombstone can be found at Jesus Chapel in Peartree Green Churchyard, near Southampton. It was erected and maintained by monies left over from Dudley and Stephens's defense fund. Its inscription reads "Sacred to the Memory of Richard Parker, Aged 17, Who Died at Sea July 25th 1884 after Nineteen Days Dreadful Suffering in an Open Boat in the Tropics, Having Been Wrecked in the Yacht Mignonette." However, it is perhaps the two biblical quotations at the end that are most telling – "Though he slay me yet will I trust in him: Job xii.15" and "Lord lay not this sin to their charge: Acts vii.60." However, although Richard Parker might have come to a grisly and early end out in the South Atlantic, his fellow mariners did not fare as well as they might have hoped.

Both Dudley and Stephens benefited from their moment in the spotlight; they were extended the coveted honor of having wax sculptures in Madame Tussauds in London. Tom Dudley, though, was anxious to get on with his life, and though he had his sailing certificate restored, he struggled to find work. Making contact with the *Mignonette*'s owner, Jack Want, he prevailed on him to subsidize his family's emigration to Australia. With the help of his wife's aunt, he set up T. R. Dudley and Co. in Sydney and enjoyed success in sail making and yacht chandlery. He was known by the locals

Figure 2.2. Richard Parker's tombstone.

as Cannibal Tom. As fate would have it, his prosperity and good fortune were short lived, as he made history a second time – he was the first Australian to die when the bubonic plague hit Australia in 1900.

Turning down Want's offer of free passage to Australia, Ed Stephens settled near Southampton and supported himself through odd jobs. Although he returned to sea on occasion, he became an alcoholic and died in poverty in Hull at the age of sixty-five in 1914. Ned Brooks avoided prison and, for a short time, traded off his fame by taking part in fairground freak shows. But he was soon back at sea. He stayed close to home and worked on the Isle of Wight ferries and died in poverty in 1919. The only one to be untroubled by the *Mignonette* disaster was, not surprisingly, Jack Want. A yacht and only several hundred pounds poorer, he was elected to the New South Wales Legislative Assembly and went on to become the state's attorney general. He died a comfortable man in 1905.

And art and law continued their dance of imitation across the years. There is much in Tom Dudley's life that is the stuff of Greek tragedy. Like Agamemnon, he made sacrifices to save himself and his sailing companions. More recently, in the award-winning novel *Life of Pi*, a sixteen-year-old Pi Patel, the son of a zookeeper, is trapped for 227 days on a twenty-six-foot lifeboat with, among other beasts, a 450-pound Bengal tiger named Richard Parker. Fortunately, that fictional Richard Parker does not get eaten, although he does himself indulge in some man eating.

Figure 2.3. Tom Dudley.

But the most startling coincidence is one of those rare occasions on which life follows art. In 1837, almost fifty years before the *Mignonette* set sail, Edgar Allan Poe published his only novella, the relatively unsuccessful *The Narrative of Arthur Gordon Pym*. The story tells of a young man who is shipwrecked along with two others. They survive for several days on the ship's floating hull but soon realize that they can survive only if one of them sacrifices himself for the benefit of the other two. After drawing lots, the cabin boy loses out and is killed and eaten. In an uncanny omen of things to come, the cabin boy's name was none other than Richard Parker.

3

Bearing Witness

In Support of the Rule of Law

I n modern societies, there are considerable feats of compromise that need to occur if a democratic government is to exist and thrive. Although power ultimately resides in the people and their representatives, it is important that this power is not exercised in a way that is willful or arbitrary. In particular, a commitment to genuine democracy demands that the majority is not permitted to ride roughshod over minorities. Any mode of responsible government, therefore, needs to maintain a series of checks and balances so that the frequently diverse and occasionally contradictory interests of different groups are maintained in political equilibrium. Among other things, this means that both popular sovereignty and political accountability must be combined in a stable and effective compact of just governance.

It often falls to the law to map out a detailed way for the ship of state to negotiate these difficult seas. This is often an unenviable task that places the courts at the very center of various political storms. In the history of democratic governance, the judges have been thrust on to center stage and have been cast in the alternating roles of heroes and villains. Indeed, as societies become more fractured and governments become less tolerated, the courts are called on, for good and bad, to be the preferred venue of last resort. Less actors and more authors, they rewrite society's constitutional and institutional script as they follow it. A key notion at the heart of these engagements is the Rule of Law. On its fiftieth anniversary, a Canadian case points up the challenges and pitfalls to be faced in ensuring that this vital, if contested, principle of political democracy retains its relevance and bite.

The Canadian province of Québec has always been a vibrant society in which matters of religion, politics, and law have enjoyed an always-dynamic and often-controversial relationship. The need to preserve and enhance its distinct identity as Canada's sole Francophone province has been paramount; it has led to several curious and fractious institutional alliances. Although a formally secular state, there was, until the Quiet Revolution of the 1960s, a very tight connection between its political and religious centers of power. It is no exaggeration to say that the history and fortunes of Québec politics and the Roman Catholic Church have been

Figure 3.1. Frank Roncarelli.

intertwined since Canada's confederation in 1867. This special feature of Québec life was never more on display than
in the immediate postwar years. The fate of political parties and the religious establishment seemed to be combined
in a series of controversial events that centered on a true
cause célèbre between the powerful Maurice Duplessis and
the proud Frank Roncarelli.

Figure 3.2. Maurice Duplessis.

Maurice Duplessis had swept back into power in the
August 1944 election. He was the leader of the Union
Nationale, a conservative party that emphasized Québec's
autonomist and nationalist agenda. After a spell in government from 1936 to 1939, Duplessis and his party had been
returned to government with fewer votes than the Liberals but with substantially more seats. This was to begin
a period which saw Duplessis remain in power as premier

for the following fifteen years and four elections. This era in Québec politics was as polarized and as hostile as any before or since. Although there is now a certain revisionism at work, it is generally regarded as La Grande Noirceur, or the Great Darkness, in which corruption, patronage, and influence mongering were the order of the day.

Loved and feared in equal measure, Maurice Le Noblet Duplessis was simply known as Le Chef. The son of a judge and politician from Trois-Rivières, he was not a modest man. He ruled Québec with an autocratic spirit and treated it as his own fiefdom – "I am the one who makes history in Québec. I am the Boss." A Roman Catholic by upbringing and a lawyer by training, he was a boozy bachelor who lived a full, if secretive, social life; he never gave an interview throughout his entire career. He was the caricature of the bully-boy politician; a more extreme version of Silvio Berlusconi would be his latter-day incarnation.

His first term in office before the Second World War produced little that was memorable. However, in 1937, the Duplessis government gave a sign of what was to come. He always and astutely appreciated the benefit of having a good enemy – so much so that he was willing to demonize whomever served his broader political ambitions and deflected attention from his own shortcomings. Playing to his rural and popular support, he enacted the so-called Padlock Law, which was officially subtitled an "Act to protect the Province Against Communistic Propaganda." As was apparent, its purpose was to rally support by targeting and fueling the perceived threat of communism or Bolshevism (as well as other troublesome organizations, like the left-wing United Jewish Peoples' Order). This piece of opportunistic legislation was ultimately struck down by the Supreme Court of Canada as being outside the province's constitutional powers. But it proved a good political strategy that bolstered Duplessis's image as a strong and fiercely pro-Québecois leader.

In 1945, Premier Duplessis consolidated his power still further by appointing himself to the portfolios of provincial attorney general and minister of intergovernmental affairs. He perpetuated a long-running battle with the federal government in Ottawa over funding, subsidies, and the provincial right to collect personal and corporate income taxes, as well as inheritance and gasoline taxes. Totally secure in his power base, he began to indulge his taste for pork-barrel politics. His extensive program of public works – highway, hospital, school, and university construction projects, as well as ambitious hydroelectric power plans – extended his personal stature and ensured the necessary (and often illicit) electoral funding of those businesses that came to be in his personal and political debt. These dubious and often-outright corrupt practices went largely unchecked in Québec, even if roundly condemned in the rest of Canada. In short, the Québec of the immediate postwar years was a place where what Duplessis wanted, Duplessis got. And it was a rare individual who had the temerity and moxie to stand up to him and his well-greased government machine.

Frank Roncarelli was that man. Born in Italy, Franco Roncarelli immigrated to Canada with his parents at the turn of the century. His father had opened the Quaff-Café on Montreal's Crescent Street in 1912. On his retirement, Frank had taken over and had become a successful restauranteur of local renown; the restaurant was a respectable and popular place with its own liquor license. In its thirty-four years' existence, there had been no trouble with the authorities. However, on a busy Wednesday lunchtime on December 4, 1946, all that changed. The restaurant was raided by police who informed Roncarelli that his liquor license had been revoked, that he was serving drinks to his patrons illegally, and that about $5,000 worth of liquor was to be confiscated. Roncarelli had made the mistake of crossing the dictatorial Duplessis.

Frank Roncarelli was a Jehovah's Witness, an evangelical Christian group that believes the present world order will soon end in Armageddon and that, upon Christ's second coming, its chosen members will be saved and elevated to heaven. An important part of their religious commitment is proselytization; they undertake persistent door-to-door campaigns to spread the word through publications like *The Watchtower* and *Awake!*. With their implacable opposition to military service (and blood transfusions), they were considered not only an eccentric fringe but also a potentially subversive force. In so many ways, they played into the hands of those mainstream Québecois who had a leaning toward persecution.

As opponents of conscription, the Witnesses' activities had been banned under the federal War Measures Act. However, once the war was over, they resumed their in-your-face campaign to convert more Montrealers to their resurrectionist movement. As far as they were concerned, they had a civic right as well as a religious duty to go about their work as domestic missionaries: the Québec Freedom of Worship Act and the charter of the city of Montreal were seen as statutory confirmations of their entitlement to distribute their literature and visit homes without municipal license. This boldness only raised further suspicion and increased hostility among Québec's Roman Catholic majority. Identified as antipapists, the Witnesses and the Catholics were on a collision course. Witnesses' meetings were disturbed, and individual Witnesses were beaten. Rather than protect the Witnesses, the government turned a blind eye.

However, as matters escalated, the authorities started to take a more active stance. As were the Communists, Jehovah's Witnesses were a convenient and easy target for Duplessis; his government began what Duplessis termed "un guerre sans merci." Under central orchestration, a favorite ploy of municipal governments was to arrest and rearrest hundreds of Witnesses on the ground that they were violating city bylaws; these curtailed the distribution of pamphlets and texts without a license and prohibited the interference with pedestrian traffic. In Montreal, the maximum fine for each such violation was $40 and costs or sixty days of imprisonment.

As a conscientious Witness, Frank Roncarelli refused to stand by while his fellow worshipers were harassed and maltreated. As one of the few relatively wealthy Witnesses, he threw his support behind the group's persecuted members. His major role was to post bail for those who had been arrested. Over three years, he had supplied property bonds for more than 390 fellow Witnesses. However, on November 12, 1946, the chief attorney of the Recorder's Court in Montreal had determined that Roncarelli's property bonds were no longer an acceptable form of security; the amount of bail was raised to up to $300 and cash was required. He ceased to post bail. But he had become identified (incorrectly but fittingly) by Duplessis and his cronies as Montreal's "self-styled leader of the Witnesses." Labeled as audacious, provocative, and a threat to law and order, Roncarelli was targeted for much closer attention.

Defiant and unapologetic, the Montreal Witnesses reacted in the only way possible to these official efforts to still their voices and their faith – by printing and distributing a pamphlet, titled "Québec's Burning Hate for God and Christ and Freedom Is the Shame of All Canada." This was what Justice Rand of the Supreme Court of Canada would later describe as "a searing denunciation of what was alleged to be the savage persecution of Christian believers." This was exactly the kind of response that Duplessis and the authorities expected. And they were ready.

The chief Crown prosecutor in Montreal, Oscar Gagnon, took swift measures to prevent the distribution of the pamphlet. He ordered the police to seize a stack of pamphlets stored in a local Kingdom Hall, the Witnesses' place of worship, in the nearby town of Sherbrooke. When it was discovered that this particular location had been leased for them by Roncarelli, the prosecutor contacted Edouard Archambault, the chairman of the Quebec Liquor Commission and subsequently chief judge of the Court of Sessions of the Peace. Informed of Roncarelli's participation and aware that he had a liquor license for the Quaff-Café, Archambault phoned Duplessis for advice. Installed as attorney general as well as premier, Duplessis urged that Roncarelli's annual liquor license (which still had more than four months to run) be revoked "definitivement et pour toujours." With little delay, Archambault did the premier's bidding: the license was withdrawn and the police dispatched to Roncarelli's now illegally operating restaurant. Within six months, the Quaff-Café had to shut its doors. There was little chance for economic survival, let alone success, for a nonalcoholic bar in late 1940s Montreal.

The next day, a triumphalist Duplessis was far from troubled or shy about the actions of the police. In a statement to the *Montreal Gazette*, he expounded on the reasons for his uncompromising stand against the Jehovah's Witnesses and why he considered their pamphlets to be "of a very libelous and seditious character." As regards the specific actions taken against Roncarelli, Duplessis stated candidly:

The sympathy which this man has shown for the Witnesses, in such an evident, repeated and audacious manner is a provocation to public order, to the administration of justice and is definitely contrary to the aims of justice. . . . [Recalling his own previous decision in 1939 to cancel the liquor license of the Harmonia Club where a Nazi propaganda film was shown], the Communists, the Nazis as well as those who are the propagandists for the Witnesses of Jehovah, have been treated and will continue to be treated by the *Union Nationale* government as they deserve for trying to infiltrate themselves and their seditious ideas in the Province of Québec.

Not all Quebeckers were prepared to be silent and complicit in this high-handed and arbitrary campaign of government recrimination against the Jehovah's Witnesses. Frank Roncarelli, for one, was not going to go quietly. Armed with his unshakable religious commitment, he was determined to expose the tyrannical actions of the smug Duplessis. But Roncarelli was not alone. As so often, successful litigation requires a fortuitous combination of politics, personalities, and – of course – timing.

Exactly who found whom is unclear, but the two Franks – Roncarelli and F. R. Scott – formed a formidable partnership. If Roncarelli had a sense of having been wronged, then Scott gave legal and intellectual voice to it. In 1946, Francis Reginald Scott was already on his way to becoming a truly outstanding and renowned Canadian. A Rhodes scholar and McGill law professor, he was a founding member of the Co-operative Commonwealth Federation, a socialist-inspired and influential group, and served as its national chairman from 1942 until 1950. Something of a renaissance figure, he remains the only Canadian to be awarded both the prestigious Governor General's Award for nonfiction for his *Essays on the Constitution* in 1977 and the same award for poetry for his *Collected Poems* in 1981. As a civil libertarian and active opponent of Duplessis, he was a natural person to involve.

Roncarelli had first approached Albert (A. L.) Stein, who was a founding partner in the small Montreal firm of Stein and Stein. Both Stein and Roncarelli quickly concluded that Scott would be a great asset to have on board, once they had failed to secure the services of a French-Canadian lawyer. But Scott needed some initial persuading. This was not because of the justice of the cause: he needed no reassurance on that count. His reluctance was more technical and professional. He had never actually pleaded a case in court. Although he had been called to the Québec bar, he could not recall whether his professional dues were paid up. Nevertheless, being well versed in the principles of a possible claim, he decided to become involved. Having done so, Scott took on the case with his customary industry and intelligence. It was to be one of only four cases that he ever pleaded.

The first two attempted claims never really got off the ground. The first line of attack was against Archambault as head of the Liquor Licensing Commission. But this action against a government official required the approval of the chief justice of Québec (who also happened to be named Archambault), and he refused to give it. The alternative approach was to sue the commission as a whole. Again, such an action could proceed only with the consent of the attorney general. Not surprisingly, as the attorney general was Duplessis himself, that consent was not forthcoming. However, these two false starts would prove to be something of a godsend.

On June 3, 1947, Scott and Stein commenced the action that was to take almost twelve years to reach a final resolution. In a bold and innovative move, Roncarelli's claim was framed as a delict (tort or civil wrong) under Article 1053 of the Québec Civil Code. This was directed against Duplessis in his personal capacity rather than against the Québec government generally. This approach had the distinct political advantage of demonstrating clearly that Roncarelli and his lawyers were as interested in obtaining civic vindication as much as monetary damages. Asking for compensation in the amount of $118,741, the pleadings alleged that Duplessis had instructed the Commission to cancel Roncarelli's permit arbitrarily and without legal authority. These actions of the premier were a deliberate act of persecution against Roncarelli's religious affiliation and a vindictive reprisal against his willingness to put up bonds for his fellow Jehovah's Witnesses.

After a series of procedural motions instigated by Duplessis, the case came on for trial in the spring of 1950.

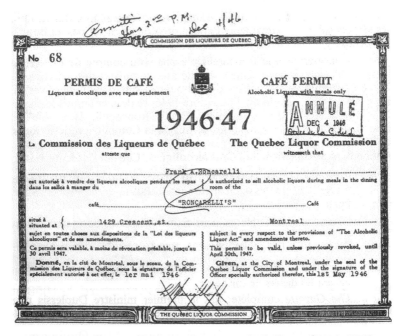

Figure 3.3. Roncarelli's permit was revoked, December 4, 1946.

Justice Gordon Mackinnon of the Superior Court deliberated for almost a year. In an unexpected judgment he found in Roncarelli's favor on May 2, 1951. He came down hard on Duplessis. In an unflinching opinion, he concluded that Duplessis was the main culprit of the piece, that he had interfered in an unauthorized and capricious way with the affairs of the Liquor Licensing Commission, that he had failed to disqualify himself from a case in which he had a personal interest, and that he had turned a legal matter (i.e., the granting of a liquor license) into a political vendetta.

Mackinnon went on to award Roncarelli damages in the sum of $8,123.53, made up of $1,123.53 for loss of value of liquor seized by the Commission; $6,000 for loss of profits from the restaurant from December 4, 1946 (the date of the cancellation of the permit) to May 1, 1947 (the date when the permit would normally have expired); and $1,000 for damages to his personal reputation. Although the actual amount recovered was relatively small, the political capital earned was large – Duplessis had lost, and his autocratic style of government was exposed for all to see.

Needless to say, Duplessis was far from finished. He appealed the judgment. In response, Roncarelli cross-appealed for greater damages. Further delay occurred, and the hearing did not come on for almost another four years. The decision of the Court of Queen's Bench (appeal side) was given on April 12, 1956. Justices Bissonnette, Pratte, Casey, and Martineau ruled against Roncarelli. They determined that the decision to cancel the permit had been made by Archambault, not Duplessis, and that Duplessis had offered only his advice. Moreover, they held that, according to the strict interpretation of Québec's Alcoholic Liquor Act, the commission was not obliged to justify before the courts the wisdom of its decisions in granting or revoking liquor permits. The only dissent was by Justice Edouard Rinfret, who twenty years later became chief justice of Québec. A day later, Duplessis dissolved the National Assembly. Two months later, he went on to increase the Union Nationale's majority and to win his record-breaking fifth and final election victory.

Unlike courts in other federal states, Canada's system of courts has a distinctly unified and centralized character. Although each province operates its own structure of courts, the judges in the superior courts are all federally appointed. As important is that all cases, whether based on provincial or on federal law, have a final right of appeal to the Supreme Court of Canada. This is a nine-person court that sits in the nation's capital, Ottawa. The appointment of those judges is made by the prime minister, but he or she is required by a combination of law and custom to select three judges from Ontario, two from the western provinces, one from the eastern provinces, and three from Québec. Although there is some deference by the non-Québec judges on appeals from Québec (as it has a civil law as opposed to a common law system), it is often the whole court that hears and decides Québec appeals. This turned out to be a matter of some political significance in Roncarelli's appeal against the province's premier.

After more delay, the case was heard by the Supreme Court of Canada for five days in early June 1958. However, since the initial revocation of Roncarelli's license in 1946, neither Duplessis nor the Supreme Court of Canada had been quiet on the matter of Québec religion and politics. In 1951, Aimé Boucher was arrested while distributing the same pamphlet that had provoked Duplessis's ire in Montreal, "Québec's Burning Hate for God and Christ and Freedom Is the Shame of All Canada."

By a narrow 5–4 majority, the Supreme Court overturned his criminal conviction for seditious libel on the grounds that peaceful modes of government criticism had to be endured in a functioning democracy. Again, in 1953, the Supreme Court faced another example of Duplessis's persecutory tactics. A Laurier Saumur had been arrested more than one hundred times for distributing Jehovah's Witness literature without official approval and in contravention of a Québec City municipal ordinance. In another 5–4 decision, the Supreme Court found against the Duplessis-influenced ordinance; the control of religion was outside the jurisdictional authority of the municipality. Although both decisions were less than decisive or resounding, the Supreme Court had begun to flex its muscles against Duplessis and his government allies.

In March 1957, the Supreme Court had finally handed down its decision on the constitutionality of the Padlock Law. In *Switzman v. Elbing and A. G. of Québec*, eight of the justices combined to declare that Québec's Act Respecting Communistic Propaganda amounted to "criminal law"; this was an exclusively federal matter and, therefore, was struck down as outside the constitutional powers of the province. Justices Rand, Kellock, and Abbott went so far as to state that the act was an unjustifiable interference with freedom of expression, which was essential under the democratic form of Canadian constitutional governance; this ruling would lay the foundation for Roncarelli's later appeal in that it showed that the court was not intimidated by the Duplessis government. The sole dissenter was Justice Robert Taschereau, who later became chief justice of Canada and then interim governor-general, Canada's head of state, for six weeks. He finessed the legal issue and upheld the law as dealing with property, not criminal law, and therefore as being within provincial authority. His judgment reinforced the view of many Quebeckers that the Supreme Court's upholding of such legal challenges was little more than Ottawa's federal meddling in Québec's provincial affairs.

When Scott and Stein went to Ottawa to argue on behalf of Roncarelli in the first week of June 1958, the odds were slightly in their favor. It was six months before the Supreme Court delivered its judgment. But on a cold January 27, 1959, Roncarelli was vindicated. In a 6–3 decision, the Supreme Court decided that his action should be maintained and his damages increased by $25,000 to the sum of $33,123.53, along with substantial interest from the date of the trial judgment and Roncarelli's legal costs. The general tenor of the decision was clear and to the point – Premier Duplessis had wrongfully and without legal justification brought about the cancellation of Roncarelli's liquor license and was liable for damages under the Civil Code. Chief Justice Kerwin and the other supporting justices did little more than confirm Mackinnon's findings and reasoning at trial; Duplessis either had no authority to intervene or, if he did, he exercised it improperly. However, in a judgment that has been given pride of place by later generations of jurists, Justice Ivan Rand gave a more expansive account in which he called on the concept of 'the Rule of Law' to support his decision against Duplessis.

A graduate of Harvard Law School and former attorney general of New Brunswick, Rand had a strong background in labor relations. He had worked for five years for the Intercolonial Railway before going to university and had been counsel for Canadian National Railways. He was appointed to the Supreme Court of Canada in April 1943. He remained there until his retirement in 1959, when he went on to serve as the University of Western Ontario's founding law dean. His judgment in *Roncarelli* was to be one of his last decisions and is considered by many to be not only one of his best but also one of the classic Canadian judgments of all time.

Although Rand's judgment lacks the sonorous quality of many leading judgments by more grandiloquent judges, it does establish for itself a quiet and impressive authority by virtue of its analytical force and legal craft. He placed Duplessis's actions in a much broader framework of public accountability than in *Boucher* or *Saumur* and laid out the parameters within which democratic officials must exercise their power. Simply because legislation appeared to confer an absolute and untrammeled discretion did not mean that officials could do as they wish and for whatever reason: they must act with reasonableness, restraint, and good faith in discharging public duty. There is always a perspective in which a statute is intended to operate; the exercise of legal power must be in accord with the statute's nature and purpose. Duplessis's actions were illegal because they were made for reasons "totally irrelevant to the sale of liquor in a restaurant." In a famous passage, Rand stated:

> [Duplessis's act] was a gross abuse of legal power expressly intended to punish him for an act wholly irrelevant to the statute, a punishment which inflicted on him, as it was intended to do, the destruction of his economic life as a restaurant keeper within the province. That, in the presence of expanding administrative regulation of economic activities, such a step and its consequences are to be suffered by the victim without recourse or remedy, that an administration according to law is to be superseded by action dictated by and according to the arbitrary likes, dislikes and irrelevant purposes of public officers acting beyond their duty, would signalize the beginning of disintegration of the rule of law as a fundamental postulate of our constitutional structure.

None of this seemed to sway the three dissenting judgments. Each gave a separate judgment whose combined thrust was that, even if Duplessis had acted improperly, there were insurmountable procedural obstacles to any successful claim by Roncarelli. For them, the fly in the ointment was that Roncarelli's lawyers did not give the required notice under Article 88 of the Québec Civil Code; all public officers were entitled to a month's notice before a claim against them was made. As Duplessis had not been given such notice, any claim by Roncarelli had no validity. The justices were of the view that the majority had not taken this condition precedent sufficiently seriously, and any efforts to argue that Duplessis was not acting in his official capacity but privately were unconvincing.

The Rule of Law, of course, is a vague and amorphous concept. And this has been part of its appeal. The basic notion has been that it should be law that governs society, not the arbitrary will of particular persons – a government of laws, not persons. In its thin version, it operates as a hedge against tyranny and high-handed governance. As a principle of legality, it seeks to ensure that government functions in a way that is more ordered and predictable than chaotic or capricious. Although this understanding seems uncontroversial in a democratic society (or any other, come to that), the Rule of Law has also been given a thick definition. The formal virtues of the thin version are supplemented by a more substantive account of democratic justice. A variety of political and moral principles are seen to be necessary to and embedded in the Rule of Law. As *Boucher* and *Saumur* suggest, these might include freedom of expression, the freedom of assembly, and other individual rights against overbearing state power. Needless to say, the appeal of this thicker version is more contested than its thinner sibling. Nevertheless, this has not prevented the courts from pushing on with incorporating parts of the thicker version into the law.

In the past fifty years or so, the *Roncarelli* decision has become a foundational building block in the development of Canada's administrative and constitutional law. It is no trite observation that, although democratically elected, the government must act in accordance with law; they have no mandate to exercise power in a purely political or arbitrary fashion. First, the executive branch of government, including not only its leading and elected officials, like Duplessis, but also the whole bureaucratic state of government departments, agencies, tribunals, and the like, must act in line with the legislative framework that grants any powers to it. On top of that, the courts have developed a body of administrative law that demands that public officials utilize those powers in a way that is reasonable and reasoned. As such, the Rule of Law has been a major device for controlling the exercise of public power and rendering it accountable between elections.

The Rule of Law has not simply been the basis of administrative law. Although that body of judge-made law can be superseded by explicit legislative language, the Rule of Law has been put into service as a significant component of Canada's developing constitutional law. In a series of decisions, the Supreme Court of Canada has determined that the Rule of Law places definite limits on the exercise of legislative as well as executive power. Although its precise scope is far from fully defined, the Court is clear that its imperatives cannot be avoided or finessed by a simple legislative enactment. Because the constitution consists of unwritten principles as well as written rules, the Rule of Law is able to play an important role. This is so even since the introduction of a constitutionally entrenched Charter of Rights and Freedoms in 1982.

The most authoritative statement of the Rule of Law's constitutional status was made in a 1998 case. Again involving Québec, it had to be decided under what conditions and circumstances the province might secede from Canada. On this obviously fraught political issue, the Supreme Court in *Re Secession Reference* took the opportunity to give a civics class in constitutional law. The Court depicted the Constitution as a quilt of formative commitments – to democracy, sovereignty, self-determination, federalism, and the Rule of Law – that interact and check one another. As such, a unanimous Court stated that "the democracy principle cannot be invoked to trump the Rule of Law." However, the judges were still a little coy about what the "highly textured" constitutional principle of the Rule of Law might mean in particular circumstances and whether it might be used offensively as well as defensively by aggrieved citizens. They were content to stress that "constitutionalism and the Rule of Law are not in conflict with democracy; rather, they are essential to it."

Many will consider the use of the Rule of Law to reign in rogue governments, like that of the autocratic Duplessis in postwar Québec, to be an exemplary instance of the courts' important and even necessary constitutional role. However, frequent judicial reliance on the Rule of Law to discipline elected government can generate its own problems. Mindful that the Rule of Law's development as part of administrative and constitutional law has been creatively engineered by courts, there is the pressing question of why the judges' definition of what does and does not count as government action that offends the Rule of Law should take precedence over that of popularly elected officials themselves. If the Rule of Law insists on a government of laws, not persons, then what makes the views of judicial persons any more acceptable than those of any other person, particularly if elected? This is a conundrum that both haunts and energizes constitutional law (see the larger discussion in Chapter 5). And it is particularly acute when the Rule of Law is given a thicker meaning and bite.

A convenient example of this is the *Roncarelli* decision itself. Whatever the view of any particular judge on whether Duplessis had acted in an entirely arbitrary and indefensible way, there was the tricky problem of what to do about the missed notice provision. It will be remembered that Justice Taschereau took the majority to task for taking an unconvincing approach to this requirement. Although not framed in such terms, his judgment could be charitably reworked as a dig at the judges in the majority that, for all their talk of high principle and the Rule of Law, they simply sidestepped a clear and valid legal provision to facilitate their own substantive disapproval of Duplessis's actions. Those judges were themselves in serious breach of the very Rule of Law that they relied on to bring Duplessis to heel: they acted with far too cavalier an attitude to the established principles of legality. In short, it was less a government of law and more one of judicial persons.

Finally, it is worth noting that in the so-called Famous Four cases – *Boucher, Saumur, Switzman*, and *Roncarelli* – the divisions among the judges were fairly predictable. In only one case did a Québec Francophone justice join the majority; this was Justice Joseph Fauteux (grandson of a Québec premier) in *Switzman*. The rest of the time, the four Québec Francophone judges, including Fauteux, dissented and would have found in favor of Duplessis or his government. Justice Robert Taschereau (son of a Québec premier) dissented in all four cases. Interestingly, the only Anglophone (bilingual) Québec judge, Justice Douglas Abbott, who was former federal minister, sided with the majority in the two cases, *Switzman* and *Roncarelli*, on which he sat. Although there is nothing determinative that can be drawn from these statistics, they do suggest that the background and political affiliation of a particular judge is far from irrelevant to their legal disposition of cases.

By the time the Supreme Court handed down its decision in January 1959, more than twelve years had elapsed since the withdrawal of the Quaff-Café's liquor license. The restaurant had long since closed, and Roncarelli, along with many other Jehovah's Witnesses, had moved to the United States.

He lived for a further twenty-two years and died in Groton, Connecticut, on September 26, 1981. Duplessis was not so fortunate. Although he managed a historic run in elected office, he was dead within seven months of the decision. His hard-living lifestyle caught up with him, and he died suddenly on September 7, 1959, at the age of sixty-eight from a massive cerebral hemorrhage in Schefferville, Québec. This marked the end of an era. The Liberals won the election the following year and the so-called Quiet Revolution began. Duplessis's style and substance of governance was abandoned and a fresh phase of politics took hold: Québec began the change to the secular and socially progressive state it has become. Whether or how much the Supreme Court's decision in *Roncarelli* and the related cases contributed to that shift remains the real stuff of historical debate.

4

In the Hunt

Power, Property, and Possession

Although law and popular opinion are not always on the closest of terms, there obviously needs to be some general congruence between the two. This is particularly true of the common law, which has developed and taken shape in the community over time. Indeed, its historical origins can be found in its efforts to distill local knowledge and custom into a more integrated body of rules for the whole community. Of course, over time, law and received wisdom tend to reinforce and track each other. The law begins to get into trouble if it strays too far from common wisdom; it can survive and command compliance only if it retains more than a nodding acquaintance with popular values. However, there are important occasions when there is no community consensus or there is a deep-seated disagreement between different groups.

These rather trite observations are especially pertinent in matters of property and ownership. Common understandings – "finders keepers; losers weepers"; "a bird in the hand is worth two in the bush"; and "a man's home is his castle" – tell us much about both popular opinion and law. There are few more foundational issues for the law to decide than what can be owned, who can own it, how can it be owned, and what it means to own something. As such, the law of property stands at the important juncture where power, commerce, social status, and common morality meet; it can be a conflicted site of community standards and expectations. An old American case about foxhunting that initially seems to have little resonance with the conditions and challenges of contemporary society captures and conveys some of those conflicts.

How do we decide who owns something? This question has long occupied the attention (and occasionally the imagination) of generations of philosophers and lawyers, from Plato to Marx and beyond. In almost all societies, there is a need to determine who gets to control and benefit a particular resource or entity; this can be a private individual, a commercial body, a local collective, the government, or the public at large. At its most broad and abstract, the issue is straightforward – once a society determines that nature can be parceled, controlled, utilized, commodified, passed on, disposed of, or whatever, how do we make those crucial first allocations? This task falls to property lawyers, whose remit covers the whole gamut from land and its resources through crafts and manufactured products to creative ideas and broadband frequencies. Although it is often treated as the most technical and dry of legal specialties, property law is perhaps the most political and controversial of them all. Beneath the complex battery of detailed rules and dense regulations, there is a rich set of choices to be made about entitlement, class, and distributive justice.

All these factors came neatly and directly into play in a small incident at the very beginning of the nineteenth century in what is now known as the Hamptons. This area of land is located on the south fork at the east end of Long Island, near New York City, and in Suffolk County; it is now a summer playground for the rich and famous. At that earlier time, it was a largely agricultural community with a population of only a few hundred. The main town was Southampton, and the events in question took place in the nearby hamlet of Bridgehampton. On its founding by the Pilgrims in the 1680s, it was a small fishing village. But today it is a very sought-after spot with the horsey set, who play polo there and host the prestigious Hamptons Classic Horse Show.

At the turn of the nineteenth century, the Southampton economy was changing and on the rise after a lengthy period of struggle. Most people in Southampton had been impoverished by the American Revolution. In the following years, farming was difficult because the soil had been depleted and the community was burdened by tax levies to pay off the war debt. The local population was largely Calvinist, and as believers in the Protestant virtues of hard work and simple living, they made light of their woes. However, as always, a select few had managed to enrich themselves. The main source of wealth was the burgeoning whaling industry and a lucrative, if dubious, trade with the slave-owning West Indies. The Post family was the beneficiary of such initiatives.

Land usage had always been contested in the Hamptons. The English Crown, the Dutch government, various tribes, original settlers, the state of New York, and town residents all made competing claims for priority over the years. This conflict was particularly heated over the town's common lands – were they primarily for traditional livestock grazing or could they be used for recreational activities by the newly arrived townsfolk? This simmering antagonism was brought close to a boil in 1768 soon after foxhunting (or, as the Americans preferred to call it, fox chasing) was introduced to Long Island.

Although it can be traced back to the Greeks and Romans, foxhunting is most closely associated with the English. Described by Oscar Wilde in his own inimitable fashion as "the unspeakable in full pursuit of the uneatable," it was a pastime indulged in by the landed gentry and by those aspiring to climb the English social ladder. Although it has some merit as a form of pest control and equestrian sport, it was and remains more a conspicuous display of social status; its functional value is small compared with its social cachet and ritualistic trappings. Unappreciated by local farmers and other landowners, basic foxhunting involves a field of scarlet-clad horse riders and specially bred hounds who track down and follow a fox wherever it may lead them, over fences, across streams, and through ditches. The whole pursuit is choreographed by a horn-blowing master of the foxhounds, who ensures that the hounds are kept on the scent of the fox; the foxhunters charge along on horseback after the marauding hounds. The fox is often lost, and a new scent has to be detected. But once the fox is cornered, it is usually the hounds who kill the unfortunate prey.

Colonial settlers brought foxhunting to the United States in the mid-eighteenth century. European red foxes were introduced in some areas specifically for foxhunting purposes. In chicken-keeping communities, like Southampton, foxes were not a welcome sight. Indeed, in 1791, the town paid a fee of four shillings for every fox killed. But there were too few foxes to make them a serious menace. Less elite than in England, American enthusiasts were more interested in the chase than the kill. However, foxhunting still required considerable resources (e.g., horses, hounds) that could be afforded by only a few. Notable earlier fox chasers were Presidents George Washington and Thomas Jefferson, who both kept packs of hounds. This tradition continued through to Jackie Kennedy and Ronald Reagan, who were both keen horse riders and occasionally joined a foxhunting jaunt. Certainly, in the early 1800s, the riders considered themselves to have free range to pursue game, regardless of ownership boundaries, across the open countryside.

In the summer of 1800, Lodowick Post was out foxhunting with some local friends, their horses, and their pack of dogs. From a family of Dutch ancestry, he was the son of Nathan Post, who was a recently arrived member of the local community. Poorly educated and from humble beginnings, the elder Post had pulled himself up by his own efforts and had made his fortune as a merchant mariner in the West Indian trade. However, he was a brusque and swaggering character who did not endear himself to his new neighbors. Considered to represent all that was dislikeable about such nouveau riche, the Post family lived in a house and a style that was brash and opulent. This stood in sharp contrast to the thrifty and puritan lives of most local residents. In such a social climate, Lodowick's decision to foxhunt was viewed as a showy and unwelcome display of extravagant living and confirmed their neighbors' low opinion of the Posts.

One of those neighbors was Jesse Pierson.* He was a young and well-regarded local schoolteacher. His family was a stalwart of the Southampton community and happily played the warranted part of educated gentleman farmers. His father was David Pierson, who was a committed Calvinist and a Revolutionary War hero. Commemorated on

---

* There is much debate over whether it is *Pierson* or *Peirson*. I have gone with *Pierson*, as this is used in the reported cases.

his tombstone as a person "distinguished for strong mental power, firmness of character and strict integrity," he had been reelected on various occasions as the community's fence viewer; he was responsible for ensuring that fences were properly located and maintained. With such a background, it was hardly surprising that the upstanding Piersons had little time for the upstart Posts. The drama that transpired over the foxhunt was an occasion on which these family scions took very predictable roles.

Lodowick Post and his accompanying field had scented a fox and were in loud chase. They were in close pursuit along the beach. What happened next was disputed and far from clear. Lodowick insisted that he was on the beach when Jesse Pierson suddenly appeared, shot the fox, and ran off with the carcass; it was apparent that Jesse knew full well that the fox was being pursued by Lodowick. Jesse told a different story. He claimed that, on his way home from teaching school, he saw that the fox had left the beach and sought refuge in an old well near Peter's Pond, a short distance from the ocean shore. He admitted that he had killed the fox and taken away its carcass but that he had done nothing wrong.

An important point of disagreement that was legally relevant was not simply the location of the land on which the killing of the fox took place but also its legal status. Lodowick insisted that he was on "wild, uninhabited, and unpossessed land" when the incident occurred and that he was fully entitled to claim the fox as his own. However, Jesse's account suggested that the killing of the fox had occurred on common land, which was used by the Pierson family and others to pasture their livestock. Although the Piersons did not own the land, they had acquired rights over it as original settlers and farmers in Southampton. Most important, the Posts had not. When Jesse refused to return the fox's carcass to Lodowick on his request, all the pieces were in place for the local dispute to move from the shore or pond to the courtroom.

Although the dispute was framed as a trivial disagreement over who owned a dead fox, the stakes were much higher. As much a clash between fathers as their sons, this was about deep divisions over property rights as well as social standing. If the Piersons were determined to defend their farming rights over Bridgehampton's common pastures and to ensure their priority over other people's recreational privileges, then the Posts were equally intent on showing that they were full members of the Bridgehampton community and that their activities were entitled to the same legal protection. It was shaping up to be a classic encounter of both legal and social significance – English versus Dutch, farmers versus entrepreneurs, and old money versus new money.

In spite of how the litigants presented their case to the courts, it turned out to be a primer on what counts as possession and how that relates to the concept of ownership – who owned the fox and had the right to kill it? Perhaps surprisingly, it was considered a novel claim; there were no compelling American or English precedents available. There were regular disputes about hunting prizes and land quarrels, but they were more often than not settled out of court; the cost and delay of litigation was prohibitive. Although Lodowick sued for the cost of the lost fox, the Posts were really suing for Jesse's interference with the hunt.

The case came on for trial on December 10, 1802. To avoid local bias, it was first heard at Justice Court in Queens County, even though the event had taken place in Suffolk County. The justice of the peace was John N. Fordham, who was a resident of Southampton, and the case was likely heard in a private home. Both Lodowick and Jesse were present and represented themselves. After a brief hearing, a six-person jury decided that the Posts had won. Although he had claimed damages in the amount of $25 (about $500 in today's money), he was only awarded $0.75 and an additional $5 toward his costs. As evidence of the underlying importance of the case to the feuding families and the neighborhood, the unusual step of appealing this minor case to the New York Supreme Court was taken; the costs of doing this far exceeded the value of the fox.

The appeal was not heard for another two years. As further proof of the importance that the case had assumed for the two families and the broader community, Jesse and Lodowick were represented by two prominent lawyers: no expense was spared. Jesse's lawyer was Nathan Sanford. A gifted advocate who had become U.S. commissioner of bankruptcy in 1802, he plied the court with references from ancient and modern learning on property. On Lodowick's side, there was David Cadwallader Colden. He had a privileged upbringing and had studied abroad in London in the mid-1780s. Very much an Anglophile, he set up his law practice in New York City and later became its mayor. Like Nathan Post (who died in October 1803), he was fascinated with sailing and sea life. Both lawyers pressed their claims' case with energy and eloquence, each playing to their own particular preferences.

No decision was made until August 1805 (when the fox or its carcass would have no longer existed). The appeal was heard by the New York Supreme Court. As it was located a fair distance away in New York City, Lodowick and Jesse did not travel with their lawyers to the proceedings. At the time, the New York courts were among the leading state courts. The judges considered themselves to have the responsibility to create a common law that would establish a legal tradition that was uniquely suited to the American milieu; it would not simply imitate the English common law. In an important deviation from standard practice, the court made no mention of William Blackstone's authoritative *Commentaries on the Laws of England*, which threw its considerable weight behind the principle of "possession of wild animals by occupancy." However, the most important feature of the appeal was that the court proceeded on the assumption that the fox had been killed on the beach, which was "waste and uninhabited ground" and not part of the common lands.

In a 2–1 decision, the Court reversed the trial decision and found in favor of Jesse Pierson: he was awarded a general sum of $121.37 (but it is unclear for what). The leading judgment was given by Associate Justice Daniel Tompkins. Appointed at the young age of thirty in 1801, he was at the beginning of his short judicial career. Tompkins went on to be a very prominent politician, becoming governor of New York in 1807 and then vice president of the United States in 1817. Revealingly, he came from a family of farmers and was quick to tell people that he was "a humble farm boy"; this could not have harmed Jesse's cause. Graduating as class valedictorian at Columbia University, Tompkins had attended lectures and come under the influence of James Kent, his fellow and supporting judge on the Pierson appeal. Kent was a more experienced judge who had become chief justice in 1804. Although Kent was still twenty years away from publishing his monumental *Commentaries on American Law*, which was to become the most influential legal tome of its time, he was already settling on and disseminating his legal opinions. In his later *Commentaries*, he came down strongly in favor of first possession and cites the *Pierson* case as his authority.

Justice Tompkins's judgment is long on principle and policy and short on legal precedent. He makes extensive reference to the scholarly literature, from the Roman Justinian through the German Puffendorf to the English Bracton, to defend his position that "a fox is an animal *ferae naturae* and that property in such animals is acquired by occupancy

Figure 4.1. James Kent (American National Biography Online).

only." Although he does not go so far as to insist that actual physical possession is required, he does maintain that "pursuit alone vests no property or right in the huntsman; and that even pursuit, accompanied with wounding, is equally ineffectual for that purpose, unless the animal be actually taken." Seeking to establish a rule that was as clear as it was straightforward, Tompkins concluded that possession was the determinant of ownership in such situations and that, as Lodowick did not have the fox in his possession but only in his sights, he had not assumed its ownership. Even though foxhunting was a socially beneficial enterprise and Jesse had conducted himself in an "uncourteous or unkind" way, the fox was killed by him, and therefore, he became its owner through his possession.

The dissenting judgment was delivered by (Henry) Brockholst Livingston. He was from a rich and powerful family who owned a half a million acres in upstate New York. As a young man, he had survived an assassination attempt but later himself killed a man in a duel. He had three wives and fathered eleven children. A classmate of future president James Madison, Livingston was a prolific judge who, in a span of four years, would pen more than 140 judicial opinions. A year after the *Pierson* decision, he was appointed to the U.S. Supreme Court. Two distant cousins – George Bush and George W. Bush – confirmed the continuing power of the family dynasty.

His judgment was something of a tongue-in-cheek affair. He scoffed at Tompkins's reliance on learned texts and thought that the dispute should have been left to "the arbitration of sportsmen" and "existing custom." He portrayed the fox as a *hostem humani generis* ("the enemy of all the world") and Jesse as a "saucy intruder." Also keen to establish a uniquely American rule, Livingston maintained that people like Lodowick who make it their business to rid the community of a genuine pest and invest their own

Figure 4.2. Brockholst Livingston (Source: The Supreme Court Historical Society).

private funds (e.g., keeping horses, breeding hounds) to
that effect are entitled to the proceeds of their effort. Certainly, the foxhunters had a superior claim than those, like
Jesse, who "had not shared in the honours or labours of
the chase . . . [and might] bear away in triumph the object
of pursuit." Accordingly, he held that the pursuit itself was
sufficient to give Lodowick constructive possession of the
fox; there was no need for actual physical possession.

And so the case was concluded. The Piersons no doubt felt vindicated. But the Posts did not leave the courts empty handed. Even though they lost the fox, they were still free to continue their foxhunting. And the familiar rivalry between the farmers and the visiting rich in the Hamptons has convincingly and long been won by the Jay Gatsbys and Carrie Bradshaws (of *Sex and the City* fame) of this world. But the significance of the case extended far beyond the confines of the Southampton environs. Abandoning accounts of property rights that were overly abstract and based on fictional notions of consent and natural rights, the New York courts had laid down a very practical account of what it means to acquire ownership of previously unowned things. It was left to later judges and jurists to work through the implications of the notion that physical possession is the origin of property and *prima facie* evidence of ownership.

In the two centuries since *Pierson v. Post*, efforts to develop the law have been marked by a tension between two competing ideas. On the one hand, there is the notion of *animus possidendi*, which recognizes the claims of those who exhibit a strong intention to possess the property in dispute. On the other hand, there is the idea of *factum possidendi*, which recognizes the claims of those who have actual physical control over the property. It will be frustrating to many to learn that the law has not bothered to develop any uniform or simple formula by which to determine possession. Indeed, the courts have left the rules deliberately vague so that what amounts to a sufficient act of possession and often resulting ownership will remain very much a contextual decision on the available evidence. However, it remains the case that possession more often than not functions as a baseline for ownership.

In many situations, the courts are not required to determine absolute ownership. Instead, what is needed is a finding of relative title to property between two parties; it is sufficient if one person is found to have a better right to possession than another person, whether that person has ultimate ownership or not. A favored method that helps prioritize peoples' property rights is the *Pierson*-style rule "first in time, first in right." This looks to the more manageable issue of temporal possession than to any more abstract inquiry about ownership. Consequently, all other things being equal (or *ceteris paribus*, as lawyers like to say), the law allocates property rights on the basis of the time of acquiring the right; the first person in time to possess the property is assumed to have the superior title. Of course, this means that present physical possession will not always trump all claims based on earlier possession.

The *Pierson* case is still the leading American authority on establishing the ownership of wild animals. To establish a legal right to possession, a person must have deprived the animal of its natural liberty and subjected it to unambiguous control; escape must not be possible. For instance, in a later English case in 1844, the court awarded possession of a school of mackerel not to the fishermen who had tracked and nearly enclosed the fish in their nets but to a later-arriving crew of fishermen who had penetrated the nearly enclosed area and actually netted the fish. Again, in a Canadian case about seal hunting in Newfoundland in 1884, it was not enough that the seals were killed and marked to establish possession against an intervener: the original killer had to be near the carcasses to prevail against an adverse possessor. If an animal escapes, ownership is lost unless the animal has a habit of returning (e.g., bees, pigeons). Of course, none of this applies to pets, which are their owners' property.

However, there has been another line of cases in which the courts have refused to grant possession to the person who has physical control. Instead, the courts have given more weight to Justice Livingston's dissent in *Pierson* that a determination of ownership should take into account local and established custom; he had argued that a decision in favor of Jesse would offend the custom of the local hunters in Long Island. For instance, in a Massachusetts case in 1881, the court granted possession of a beached whale not to the person who found it on the beach, but to the hunter who had harpooned it days earlier and was waiting for it to turn up onshore; this better reflected the local custom, which was considered essential to the profitable operation of the whaling industry. However, custom will prevail only when its application is recognized by the entire industry and when the practice is regularly followed and approved. This means that the custom exception to *Pierson*'s possession rule will apply only in a limited set of circumstances.

Today, the contested ownership of wild animals is not a staple of legal disputes and court decisions. Nevertheless, the courts have tended to hold with the possession rule. A successful claimant will have to show that he or she has asserted as much control as is practicable in regard to the piece of property in question and the surrounding circumstances. For instance, the degree of control required to establish possession of a lost bracelet in an airline passenger lounge is much greater than that necessary for a shipwreck on the ocean floor. In an English case in 1958, it was held that the finder of a locked box has the intention to possess its contents even if he or she does not know what exactly lies inside the box. Likewise, a landowner was presumed to possess all items on his premises even though he did not know that they were there.

In terms of natural resources, such as oil, water, and minerals, it is still considered the common law that the first driller to tap and produce oil from a pool that underlies the land of several owners has acquired possession of the oil, even though it might well drain others' land. This has led to severe confrontations, and local statute law has often been introduced to ration exploitation and deal with inefficient overproduction. As regards riparian rights, adjacent landowners are entitled to make reasonable use of the river or lake. When there is insufficient flow to meet the needs of all owners, usage is usually allocated in proportion to the length of frontage owned; there are special rules for discharging materials into the water. Riparian rights also include the right to use the water for recreational purposes and for docking and navigation.

As society has become more sophisticated and ownership more valuable, there has been a greater willingness to recognize more and more things as property and, therefore, capable of being owned. As well as deciding that some things cannot be property (e.g., slaves, wives), there are famous cases over genetically modified seeds and even laboratory mice. Apart from real property (which includes all rights in regard to land), there are different kinds of personal property that are divided into so-called tangibles (e.g., furniture, bicycles, and of course animals) and intangibles (e.g., patents, financial instruments, copyrights). In such situations, property rights are generally acquired through creation; this leads to genuine contestation among competing claims. Recent cases concern increased competition over software programs, music sampling, and file sharing. To circumvent the problem of physical possession, governments have introduced a whole regime of intellectual property rights. Although there is a centralized scheme of registration, there are many limitations on what can be patented or trademarked, who gets to own it, and how it can be used.

Even if one can establish ownership of a piece of property, that does not mean that the rights that go with it are absolute or unconditional. The owners of property are not free to do whatever they want with property whenever they want. Property law is best thought of as creating a set of relationships that exist between persons and things; it creates a bundle of entitlements that some people can exercise in certain circumstances, at certain times, and under certain conditions. Again, it is about the relative priority and enforcement of rights among different claimants. Even when it comes to owning real property, owners cannot expect that their interests and desires will always be given precedence over others' interests; there are a whole host of codes, regulations, rules, and conventions that curtail the freedom and entitlements of owners. Some jurisdictions still allow hunting on unenclosed lands unless no-trespassing signs have been posted. People's homes are very rarely their castle or hunting ground.

As *Pierson* hints at but never explicitly acknowledges, possession and even ownership do not create a black-and-white set of fixed entitlements. Instead, it is better viewed as very colorful, highly shaded, and dynamic process in which the content and extent of rights obtained are fundamental but whose effect will vary over time and across contexts. In contemporary society, determining whether it is the Jesses or the Lodowicks of this world who own something is often not the end point of the legal inquiry but only one of its staging posts. The most pressing question is what follows from the fact of possession or ownership – can you do whatever you want with the fox and its contemporary equivalents?

More than two hundred years later, there are still eccentric incidents that challenge our understandings of property law. A good example comes from the popular world of baseball, a far cry from the elite indulgence of foxhunting. When Barry Bonds of the San Francisco Giants hit his record-breaking seventy-third home run into the right-field stands of the Pac Bell Park during the 2001 baseball season, it was initially caught by a fan, Alex Popov, in his baseball mitt. A melee ensued and another fan, Patrick Hayashi, came up with ball. Hayashi left the game with the ball and put it in a safety deposit box. Realizing the ball was likely worth a small fortune, Popov sued Hayashi and claimed that he had a prior property claim as he was the first to possess it. Judge Kevin McCarthy reached a judgment that was equally praised and lambasted for its Solomonic qualities. He held that, although the ball initially belonged to Major League Baseball, it was effectively abandoned and unpossessed when it left the field of play. However, as Popov had only momentarily caught the ball, this did not give sufficient possession to establish physical control of the ball. Therefore, in a significant variation from the *Pierson* decision, Hayashi was found to have taken the more secure possession of the ball and was its legal owner.

Yet the judge was not finished. To deter antisocial behavior of Hayashi's "bleacher" kind, he decided that Popov and Hayashi would each would get half the proceeds from any sale; ownership was not an all-or-nothing matter. The ball was eventually auctioned for the staggering amount of $450,000 to comic-book creator Todd McFarlane. No doubt, both Jesse and Lodowick (and the fox) would have all turned over several times in their graves.

5

Shades of Brown

A Constitutional Catharsis

There are many debates that go on in and around law. As these great cases reveal, courts are some of the regular sites for the informed discussions that occur about the way the law and public policy should develop and grow. Although these exchanges are important dimensions of the law's operation, perhaps the more crucial debates are about the legitimate role of the courts in being so engaged in actually shaping law and public policy. For many, of course, this creative function will jar with their political understanding that, in societies that pride themselves on being democratic, judges are supposed to apply the law, not create it wholesale. This is especially so in matters of constitutional law, where legislative and executive institutions cannot correct quickly or easily, if at all, the decisions of the judicial branch of government. Others defend the courts as being necessary partners in the democratic governance of society; judges are less prone to succumb to political expediency and more likely to remained principled in their deliberations and decisions.

This underlying debate about the limits of judicial power and the correct method to be used by them is nowhere more heated and intense than it is in the United States. As regards the decisions of its Supreme Court, there is almost as much scrutiny of the nine judges' style and approach to fulfilling their institutional responsibilities as there is of the substance of the individual decisions made. The judges must not only grapple with the difficult issues that come before them but also do so in a way that gains the approval of their observers and critics. And this task is no more evident or demanding than in the Court's handling of race and racism. The Supreme Court's decision in *Brown* is one of its most controversial and famous; it was the judicial shot heard around the world. It is still considered a litmus test for opposing views about the legitimate approach to 'proper' constitutional adjudication.

Linda Brown was an eight-year-old girl in the third grade of elementary school in Topeka, Kansas. She lived with her parents and sister in Shawnee County. Her father was a Santa Fe Railroad employee and a part-time assistant pastor at his local St. John Methodist Episcopal Church. She often walked to school. Sumner Elementary only was seven blocks from her house. However, Linda had to walk through a railway switchyard or occasionally take a bus to Monroe Elementary, which was more than a mile and twenty-one blocks from her home. She was not allowed to attend Sumner School because she was black, so she had to attend the segregated Monroe School. Ironically, Sumner School was named after the famed abolitionist Charles Sumner.

Race and education was a highly contested relationship in midcentury America. In the Southern states especially, segregation was an established fact of life. Yet things were beginning to change at midcentury. For instance, whereas seventeen Southern states mandated racial segregation and four others permitted local districts to impose it, sixteen other states actually prohibited it. In Kansas (where about 8 percent of the population were African American), there was segregation, but it was not universal. Black people were allowed in some of the same civic organizations as whites, and they were not forced to ride in the back of buses. Most of the downtown public facilities were segregated by practice, if not by law. High schools were not segregated, but they had separate extracurricular activities, like athletics and prom dances, and teachers (who were largely white) policed an informal segregated social system. As for elementary schools, they were segregated, although their funding was not as unequally funded in Topeka as in many school districts.

Of course, there had been robust and continuing challenges to these practices. One of the best-known and effective organizations in this struggle was the National

Association for the Advancement of Colored People
(NAACP). It had been founded in 1909 as a biracial civil
rights group led by the legendary African American, W. E. B.
DuBois, and was committed to eliminating racial discrimination in all its manifestations; it is still going strong
today. In the 1930s, the NAACP began its national campaign to challenge segregation in public education through
the courts under the leadership of the Harvard-educated
attorney Charles Hamilton Houston; he had become the
head of the all-black Howard University law school in 1929
and earned a reputation as "the Man Who Killed Jim Crow."
Along with a coterie of talented young lawyers, Houston
began to litigate cases that sought to demonstrate that the
separate-but-equal interpretation of the Constitution's guarantee of equal protection in the Fourteenth Amendment, as
laid down in the Supreme Court's ruling in *Plessy v. Fergu-
son* in 1896 (upholding segregated facilities in railway cars),
was bad constitutional law.

After the Second World War, there was an increased
push against discrimination. Despite fierce resistance in the
South, the civil rights movement was gaining real momentum. Significantly, it had attracted vital government support under the presidency of Harry Truman: he had signed
executive orders that ended segregation in the military
and mandated equal opportunity in federal employment.
Although the NAACP lawyers suffered several significant
setbacks, especially in Tennessee and Louisiana, their litigation against segregated schooling was coming good and

bringing serious benefits. By 1952, the NAACP had successfully litigated thirty-four of its thirty-eight civil rights cases across the country: its membership had grown to around five hundred thousand. As Linda Brown walked to school in 1950, she would have had no idea that she was about to become a national and historical icon in the struggle against segregated schooling and race discrimination generally.

In 1950, the Topeka branch of the NAACP, led by McKinley Burnett (in whose honor the school board's administration building is now named), turned its attention to an 1879 Kansas law. This permitted cities with a population of fifteen thousand to maintain separate school facilities for so-called Negro and white students. After much local door-to-door campaigning, a group of thirteen parents was found who agreed to be plaintiffs on behalf of their twenty children. It was to be the twelfth case filed in Kansas that sought to end segregation in public schools. Oliver Brown, Linda's father, was not the first named plaintiff; this was in fact the unrelated Darlene Brown who was alphabetically prior. But the NAACP determined that it would be more strategically effective to have a man with a nuclear family than have someone who was a single, female parent as the lead litigant. Although this was understandable, it also suggested that the fight against racism was to take definite precedence over any immediate appreciation of gender discrimination.

As directed and agreed, in the fall of 1950, Oliver Brown sought to enroll Linda at the nearby white Sumner School.

Figure 5.1. Oliver Brown.

After much arguing and shouting with the school principal, he was rebuffed in no uncertain terms and directed to take Linda back to the more distant black Monroe School. As Linda Brown herself would later reminisce:

> We lived in an integrated neighborhood and I had all of these playmates of different nationalities. And so when I found out that day that I might be able to go to their school, I was just thrilled, you know. And I remember walking over to Sumner school with my dad that day and going up the steps of the school and the school looked so big to a smaller child. And I remember going inside and my dad spoke with

someone. . . . I could hear voices and hear his voice raised, you know, as the conversation went on. And then he immediately came out of the office, took me by the hand and we walked home from the school. I just couldn't understand what was happening because I was so sure that I was going to go to school with Mona and Guinevere, Wanda, and all of my playmates.

The case was brought by three local lawyers, Charles Bledsoe, Charles Scott, and John Scott, who were assisted by Robert Carter and Jack Greenberg of the NAACP Legal Defense and Educational Fund. The main thrust of the case was simple and straightforward – there could be no equality as long as schools were organized on the basis of race; segregated schooling perpetuated and placed a stigma of inferiority on African American children. It was a bold and uncompromising challenge that, along with the shifting sensibilities of the times, had the potential to revolutionize race relations in the Southern United States and beyond.

On August 3, 1951, a three-judge district court panel entered judgment against Linda Brown and the other children. Upholding the 1879 Kansas law, the court held that segregation in public education did have a detrimental effect on black children but denied relief on the ground that the facilities in the two sets of schools were comparable in terms of the buildings, transportation, curricula, and educational qualifications of teachers. However, in a finding that was to assume great significance later, the judges allowed psychological evidence that African American children were adversely affected by segregation to become part of the official record. Under a federal statute, the case went on direct appeal to the Supreme Court of the United States, where it was combined with three other cases from Delaware, South Carolina, and Virginia. Before the appeal could be heard, the Topeka Board of Education announced that it planned to desegregate the schools. But the Supreme Court announced that, unless the state of Kansas was willing make a binding declaration that its segregated system of education was unconstitutional and invalid, the case would have to proceed. The state refused to adopt such a public resolution.

Arguments were first heard by the Supreme Court on December 9, 1952, and the following two days. Robert Carter represented Linda, and Assistant Attorney General Paul Wilson appeared on behalf of a half-hearted Kansas that had to be prodded several times by the Supreme Court before it put in a defense. It was also Wilson's first argument in any appellate court, state or federal. However, mindful that this was a combined appeal, the main confrontation was between Thurgood Marshall and John Davis in *Briggs v. Elliott*, the companion South Carolina case on school desegregation. Both were at the top of their game, and for both, this hearing was to be one of the defining moments of their litigation careers.

Thurgood Marshall was a colossus of the law. The grandson of a slave, he was the NAACP's lead counsel and had been for more than ten years; he went on to become the nation's first black Supreme Court judge. Born into a middle-class Baltimore family in 1908 (and soon shortening his unwieldy given name from *Thoroughgood*), he had been refused entry into the University of Maryland law school because of his race. Instead, he went to the all-black Howard University, where he starred and was mentored by its dean and NAACP stalwart, Charles Houston. He had an astounding record of success before the Supreme Court, winning twenty-nine of thirty-two cases argued. In *Brown*, he argued steadfastly and eloquently that the time had come to reverse *Plessy* and to fulfill the full emancipatory promise of the Constitution's Fourteenth Amendment.

Across the podium was the dogged John W. Davis. Then seventy-nine years old, he had been the U.S. solicitor general (a position that Marshall was to fill a little more than a decade later) and a Democratic presidential candidate in 1924. A veteran of a formidable 250 Supreme Court appearances, he was personally committed to the rightness of the states' cause and took the case for free as a personal favor to South Carolina's governor, James Byrnes. The main thrust of his argument was that the states had the constitutional right, other things (e.g., resources, facilities) being equal as they were in Topeka, to enact legislative plans for education based on race and that the NAACP's case went to the wisdom of legislative policy, not the validity of constitutional law. *Brown* was to be one of his last cases. After he died the next year, some speculated that his participation in *Brown* sapped his spirit and contributed to his demise.

It was no secret that the nine Supreme Court judges were divided over the school desegregation case. Four justices hailed from the South – Hugo Black of Alabama, Tom Clark of Texas, Stanley Reed, and Chief Justice Fred Vinson, both of Kentucky – and were expected to side with Kansas against Linda Brown. At the very least, it would have to be very canny judgment to persuade them to sign on and support Linda and the NAACP's side over that of the states. At the behest of Felix Frankfurter, the only Jew on the Court, it was decided to hear rearguments; he knew that a 5–4 pro-integration decision would be too weak to carry the political day. As well as focusing arguments on specific concerns of the judges (i.e., historical evidence of the Fourteenth Amendment, the shape of desegregation, and the precise remedy given), the added time would allow further behind-the-scenes lobbying by Frankfurter and his supporting colleagues. Reargument was set for almost one year later.

However, in the early fall, fate stepped in. Chief Justice Fred Vinson, a likely dissenter, died suddenly from a heart attack in his hotel room on September 8, 1953. Understandably, but perhaps uncharitably, Frankfurter was reputed to have said, "This is the first indication I have ever had that there is a God." President Dwight Eisenhower appointed

Earl Warren as Vinson's successor both to the Court and to the chief judgeship. He was a former California governor and had supported the state's internment of Japanese Americans in the War. In 1948, he was on the losing Republican ticket when he ran as Thomas Dewey's vice presidential candidate. Although not considered as conservative as Vinson, Warren's appointment seemed to suggest it would be business as usual at the Supreme Court. But Warren was to confound his fellow Republicans and become the most liberal court leader in American judicial history: the Republican Eisenhower would later concede that his nomination was "the biggest damn fool mistake."

Reargument occurred on December 7, 1953, the twelfth anniversary of Pearl Harbor. Before a standing-room-only crowd, Marshall and Davis resumed battle. The emphasis was on whether the ratifiers of the Fourteenth Amendment in 1868 intended to prevent racial segregation in schools. They each took entirely predictable positions. After three days of intense exchanges, the judges of the Supreme Court took five months to deliberate and delivered their judgment on May 17, 1954.

That Monday was quite a judgment day for many reasons. Justice Robert Jackson came directly from the hospital at which he had been convalescing for a couple of months since a serious heart attack. Justice William Douglas was honored in his chambers with an award from the American Foot Health Association for his efforts to preserve a 185-mile Chesapeake & Ohio Canal towpath from being turned into a highway. The justices took their seats at the Supreme Court bench at noon. The courtroom was packed to capacity, including all the Supreme Court's clerks and Justice Jackson's doctor. First, 119 attorneys were admitted to practice before the Supreme Court. The justices then read out the Court's decisions of the day. Four decisions were rendered before the main item of business was reached. At about 12:40 p.m., Chief Justice Warren began to read his opinion for the Court in Case Number One on that term's docket, *Oliver Brown et al. v. Board of Education of Topeka, Shawnee County, Kansas*, along with its companion cases from South Carolina, Virginia and Delaware.

In his measured tones, Chief Justice Warren read out a unanimous judgment on behalf of the Court in favor of Linda Brown and the other children. He concluded that "separate educational facilities are inherently unequal" and "violate the Fourteenth Amendment to the U.S. constitution which guarantees all citizens equal protection of the laws." Although the judgment carefully confined itself to education, it was a landmark victory for the NAACP and African Americans. Yet there was much that was not said; this would have a significant effect on its immediate reception and later developments.

It was a very brief judgment considering the importance of the issue; it ran to only eleven pages as compared to a more standard length of forty or fifty pages. It seemed that, to secure the support of all nine judges, the chief justice's judgment was deliberately short on legal argument and long on sociological imperatives. Also, Warren later insisted that he wanted the opinion published in its entirety in the daily newspapers so he had written it in terms that ordinary people could understand.

Rather than cite constitutional text or legal precedent, Warren chose to rely on statistical and scholarly analyses of race and education; as much weight was given to Gunnar Myrdal's 1944 *An American Dilemma: The Negro Problem and Modern Democracy* as the Court's own jurisprudence. Great emphasis was placed on the evidence in the initial district court record that, even though resources might be equally allocated to the schools, separate schooling was psychologically damaging to black children. There was no ringing endorsement of high moral principle and no condemnation of racism and racial discrimination more generally. The hope was that blandness combined with brevity would be more effective at appeasing the South. As history would show, this was a forlorn gesture.

The immediate response to *Brown* was mixed. There were as many who hailed it as an abomination as those who called it a triumph. Once its sweeping significance was appreciated, many Southern politicians and commentators condemned the decision and referred to May 17, the day when the decision was handed down, as Black Monday: a National Association for the Advancement of White People (NAAWP) was actually founded. However, there were those in the establishment, including the president, who hailed the decision as truly epochal in its timeliness and effect. As

Figure 5.2. Woman and daughter after High Court ruling.

membership in the NAACP surged, Thurgood Marshall predicted that school segregation would be completely abolished
within five years. However, as important as the *Brown* decision was, it took much longer; a breakthrough in civil rights
only occurred after much further time and struggle.

In *Brown*, the court had deliberately sidestepped the
question of how desegregation could and should be brought
about. Accordingly, after hearing further argument, the
Supreme Court handed down *Brown II* in May 1955. Stress-
ing that there would need to be different solutions in
different local school districts depending on the particular organization of schooling there, the court again rendered a unanimous judgment. The chief justice urged school
boards to end segregation and integrate schools "with all

Figure 5.3. George E. C. Hayes, Thurgood Marshall, and James M. Nabrit, following the Supreme Court decision ending segregation.

deliberate speed" (a phrase he borrowed from Francis Thompson's poem "The Hound of Heaven"). Unfortunately, various Southern school boards saw this as an opportunity to drag their feet; a variety of tactics, including token integration and the public financing of private white schools, were deployed. A protracted phase of desegregation began that would take decades to administer and bring to anything like a satisfactory conclusion. Indeed, like Dickens's case of

Jarndyce v. Jarndyce in his *Bleak House*, it is a process that continues and "still drags its dreary length before the court" and the salons of public opinion.

Brown is one of a handful of cases that almost everyone agrees has a special place in the American constitutional tradition. However, beyond that general fact, there is little agreement. Its judgment, the doctrinal basis of the decision, and its academic and popular reception all still remain hotly contested. In its rhetorically bland but politically explosive judgment, the unanimous Supreme Court held that the inconclusive nature of the 1868 Fourteenth Amendment's history obliged it to take notice of the contemporary state of public education and strike down *Plessy*'s separate-but-equal doctrine. But *Brown* placed the workings of the Supreme Court under an extraordinarily glaring public spotlight. Difficult questions were being asked inside and outside the legal community about the legitimacy of the courts as constitutional arbiters. Had the Supreme Court sold its legal soul to follow its political heart?

As do many other democracies, the United States has a written and aging Constitution that places very definite limits on what legislative bodies can or cannot do. Because that Constitution is not at all easy to amend or alter, the authority to determine what the Constitution's general guarantees and commitments mean is very great: What does equality require? What amounts to due process of law? And what is free speech? Those bodies that are entrusted with such responsibility are under a great pressure to demonstrate that their formidable power is exercised in a legitimate manner. In particular, where power is placed in the people, it is vital to ensure that those entrusted with such final authority, especially if unelected and unrepresentative, do not simply translate their own personal political preferences into law. As in the United States, this power and responsibility has fallen to the judges in most democracies.

In the overheated world of constitutional law, there are almost as many theories of constitutional interpretation as there are jurists and judges. However, there are two basic camps. There are those (let us call them the "past-ists") who are backward looking and find meaning in the original words and/or intentions of the Constitution's creators; they maintain that the justice of those discovered meanings are not the concern of judges but of those with power to amend the Constitution. For them, constitutional law is a relatively static affair. On the other side, there are those (let us call them the "present-ists") who insist that the Constitution is not stuck in the past and must be capable of organic growth if is to retain its superior authority; society must be governed by a sense of justice that is in step with the times and not be governed by the dead hand of the distant past. For them, constitutional law is an organic work-in-progress.

So, in *Brown*, although the Court's terse judgment tried to sidestep the larger questions of constitutional legitimacy, this maneuver only served to underline them. Any rejoicing in the substantive result was matched only by the lamentation at its inadequate basis in constitutional doctrine and reasoning. Indeed, the *Brown* decision points up the classic tension in constitutional adjudication. In general terms, it pits the past-ists against the present-ists in the challenge to avoid reducing adjudication to what Chief Justice Taney, in the reviled 1857 *Dred Scott* decision (which denied slaves and their descendants constitutional rights and precipitated the Fourteenth Amendment) termed "the mere reflex of the popular opinion or passion of the day" – if there is a move beyond the framers' intent, what is the source that judges should use to inform and limit their decisions?

In reality, few judges take a fundamentalist position, and most try to balance out the pushes of contemporary values and pulls of historical tradition; they are not quite past-ists and present-ists by turn, but they resist easy categorization. Although the present-ists face the more obvious and stiffer challenge of maintaining a distinction between law and politics, the past-ists are no less implicated in this debilitating dilemma. Not only are the availability, applicability, and acceptability of original meanings far from obvious or technical matters, but also there is the broader political challenge of explaining what makes it any more just or proper for contemporary society to be governed by yesterday's values than today's. In short, notwithstanding that the Supreme Court in *Brown* found the meaning of the Fourteenth Amendment's guarantee of equal protection to be inconclusive: what evidence is there that the founding parents intended their views, not only their words, to be decisive for future generations? And what about the courts' body of precedents that has developed over the past two hundred years?

Viewed in these terms, the decision in *Brown* points up the central dilemma in constitutional law – to demonstrate convincingly not only that *Brown* is politically right (and that *Plessy* is politically deplorable) but also that *Brown* is good constitutional law. Constitutional judges and scholars must be able to explain why something is good constitutional law apart from or in addition to the fact that it is simply good politics at the time of the decision, whether they couch that conclusion in originalist terms or not. If there is no appreciable difference between good law and good politics, there seems no reason to treat judges' decisions as any more neutral, objective, or nonideological and, therefore, authoritative than political opinion at large. This is especially so where public opinion is as divided as in *Brown*'s issue of segregated schooling.

But constitutional law and politics cannot be one and the same thing as there is no one politics and, therefore, no one Constitution. The maintenance of such a law–politics distinction might be plausible in a society that shares a general consensus on political controversies. But, of course, that is not the case in American society, especially for (or perhaps because of) the constitutional cases that fall for judicial decision. As such, the legal debate over *Brown* and other controversial case like *Roe v. Wade* (upholding women's limited right of reproductive choice) is nothing less than a struggle over the soul of constitutional law; it is largely politics masquerading as interpretive theory. The fate of *Brown* as a great or not-so-great case will be determined by the contingent outcomes of political engagement. As politics goes, so goes the Constitution.

Of course, *Brown* was not entirely out of the blue: the Supreme Court had begun to chip away at the *Plessy* doctrine over the previous couple of decades in cases like *Missouri ex rel. Gaines*, *Sweatt v. Painter*, and *McLaurin*, all of which dealt with race and equality. However, the decision was far from a routine extension of existing precedent or a natural progression from established doctrine. Indeed, as mentioned, the brevity of the Court's judgment, its unanimity, and its sparse argumentative base all speak to the lengths that the Court's justices were willing to go to compromise and present a united front.

The fact is that decisions like *Brown* become great cases not because they are legally correct or analytically sound, but because they are ultimately accepted and embraced by society; their supporters ultimately triumph over their detractors. And these cases remain in that exalted position only as long their political appeal and social legitimacy can be sustained. For example, the difference between *Plessy* and *Brown* has nothing to do with their legal integrity as a matter of constitutional doctrine. It has everything to do with the changing currents and concerns in the contemporary political context. *Plessy*'s separate-but-equal dogma ceased to be a fixed point on the constitutional compass because it no longer enjoyed sufficient political confidence and public support, at least among the elite. When Justice Harlan in 1896 predicted in his dissent that the *Plessy* judgment "will, in time, prove to be quite as pernicious as the decision in *Dred Scott*," he was talking about its substantive merits as a political outcome, not its formal qualities as a legal judgment. And he was correct.

Great cases are only as authoritative as the political values that they represent. Although *Brown* is still loudly and regularly fêted, its constitutional influence has been reinterpreted in line with current (and changed) values. It has become an icon for the Constitution-is-color-blind approach; it has been used as an argument against affirmative action and even race-conscious efforts to integrate public schools. As such, the United States remains a long way from the integrationist vision that emerged from *Brown*. Indeed, *Plessy* has experienced something of a renaissance in the form of the rebellion against affirmative action initiatives: any resort to race-based categories is treated as invalid whether the motivations are progressive or regressive. This shift in the standing of *Brown* reflects the changing composition of the Supreme Court's personnel and a more conservative public attitude to race relations. As do politics and social values, constitutional law moves on; it is a little bit effect (i.e., the long-running activist drive of the NAACP) and a little bit cause (i.e., the civil rights revolution of the 1960s).

The deeper message of *Brown*, therefore, is that there is no theoretical formula that can underwrite the correctness of any particular judicial decision. Nor will judges who go in one direction rather than another be able to claim that they are acting in a more constitutionally legitimate manner than any other judge. This does not mean that there are no rational grounds for constitutional law; it simply means that there are no grounds that are final or determinative by the sheer force or rightness of their legal argumentation. As cases like *Brown* show, tenured judges can do much what they like provided that they can persuade enough of their colleagues to join them and then go on to galvanize sufficient popular support. Good constitutional law is whatever is accepted as good constitutional law. Despite what others claim or pretend, there is nothing much else to it.

The next decade or so after *Brown* was a period of increased confrontation around race and racism. For instance, on September 4, 1957, Arkansas Governor Orval Faubus called up the National Guard to surround Central High School in Little Rock to prevent black students from going in. Three weeks later, after hectic legal and political efforts, nine black students were escorted by federal troops through a cordon of protesting white families and given entrance to the school. Such confrontations were typical. Sadly, the elite of Little Rock failed to rally behind the Supreme Court's decision in

Brown. Cultivating the appearance of institutional compliance rather than a reality of racial justice, any prospect of early change was frustrated and a legacy of white flight, poor urban schools, and ingrained racism was established.

It was, of course, to be expected that the Southern establishment would not permit the institutional structures of segregation to be dismantled without a fight. However, that fight turned increasingly bloody and violent; there were brutal slayings, especially that of the young Emmett Till, and lynchings of African Americans. However, under the inspirational stewardship of Martin Luther King, Jr., there were various acts of nonviolent disobedience, including the Montgomery bus boycott, the Greensboro sit-in, and the Selma-to-Montgomery march. The introduction of the Civil Rights Act in 1964 (which banned racial discrimination in public places, even if on private property) and the Voting Rights Act in 1965 (which outlawed discriminatory voting policies and practices) were major events in both their real and symbolic impact.

School desegregation remained a hot-button issue. Segregationists in the South adopted all manner of strategies to derail the desegregation juggernaut. In extreme cases in the early 1960s, some school districts simply closed down all public schools and left families to a burgeoning private system. This, of course, meant that the poorer black community was deprived of almost any education at all. Even when the schools reopened, the white flight out of the urban centers had the effect of many inner-city schools still having a largely black student body. In the 1970s and 1980s, many school districts across the United States were obligated by the federal courts to implement mandatory busing plans whereby students were allocated to schools on the basis of racial identity, not geographic proximity, and then transported there. This initiative was highly controversial and was strenuously resisted by even those white families (and black families as well) who supported the general idea of desegregated education. This busing development was somewhat ironic in that Oliver and Linda Brown's complaint was as much about not being able to attend her local school as it was about discrimination more generally.

Events in Topeka itself were typical of what happened in the South as a response to the *Brown I and II* decisions. The initial official plan was to assign all students to their neighborhood school without attention to race. However, because neighborhoods tended to be racially defined, this had no real effect on on-the-ground segregation. This led to further litigation under the Browns' name. In accepting the Topeka plan as a "good faith effort," a unanimous U.S. district court in 1955 held that "desegregation does not mean that there must be an intermingling of the races in all school districts: . . . it means only that they may not be prevented from intermingling or going to school together because of race or color." In the early 1970s, the high schools, long formally desegregated, still had different bells for black and white students, separate black and white basketball teams, and black and white prom queens; black discontent was still running high. It took many more years before significant progress was made. And even now, Thurgood Marshall's dream of a fully integrated system of school education remains elusive.

Today, the debate around school education and race continues. Although legally sanctioned segregation may be a thing of the past, there is still substantial segregation as a matter of social reality. For instance, Mississippi's Charleston High School was officially desegregated in the 1970s but had continued to hold separate proms for black and white. It was only in 2009, after sustained efforts by the actor and local Morgan Freeman, that the first integrated prom dance occurred. School districts still work toward balancing geographic proximity and racial mix. Indeed, there is a renewed academic debate about the overlooked values of single-race (and single-gender) schooling. Relying on educational data and social analyses, some argue that visible minorities do better in less adversarial and more culture-sensitive contexts. Of course, this is both a long and short way from the *Brown* decision.

As for the Browns, the Supreme Court decision in *Brown* was as much a beginning to their legal involvement as anything else. Sadly, Oliver died of a heart attack in 1961; he had seen the end of legal segregation but not the end of segregation in public education. In 1978, a thirty-six-year-old Linda, married and named Brown Thompson, still lived in Topeka and had children of her own. After considerable persuasion, she agreed to be part of an effort to reignite the *Brown* litigation, as schooling practices were still much the same twenty-five years later. Under its policy of open enrollment, Topeka schools remained effectively segregated: about 60 percent of the children who attended their local school were still part of a segregated educational experience. Although the district court agreed to reopen the case, it denied Linda's petition and found the schools to be sufficiently integrated. Further litigation ensued. But it took until 1993 for the courts to oblige the Topeka School Board to implement a plan that would actually bring about full desegregation; new schools were opened, and the judicial standards of racial balance were achieved in July 1999. Linda's sister, Cheryl, became part of the family business; she is involved in running the Brown Foundation for Educational Equity, Excellence and Research, which was established in 1988 to pay tribute to those who participated in *Brown* and to continue its legacy. Consequently, more than fifty-five years later, the struggle still goes on.

6

A Snail in a Bottle

Nature, Neighbors, and Negligence

Over the years, observers of highbrow and popular culture have assembled a large menagerie of metaphorical pets to better their social commentary – Archilocus, and later Isaiah Berlin, befriended a wily fox who knew many things and a ponderous hedgehog who understood one big thing; the proverbial three little pigs learned to build their houses "as best they could"; the Japanese have their three wise monkeys who "see no evil, hear no evil, and speak no evil"; George Orwell created a whole farm of political animals; and Aesop put together a whole stable of fabled beasts.

Although the law cannot compete with this rich and varied brood, it does have its own favored animals. Leaving aside that lawyers themselves are often depicted in the popular imagination as snakes and weasels, one the most celebrated of these legal creatures is a small and dead Scottish mollusk. Foraying for a safe and food-rich environment, it managed to force its way into the legal world in August 1928 in a way that few would have imagined. The fact that its actual existence in these particular legal circumstances has always been in doubt only adds to its notoriety. So, along with the unfortunate fox in *Pierson* (see Chapter 4), the humble snail holds pride of place in the legal garden.

May Donoghue was in her early thirties and had lived a tough life by any standards. The daughter of a steelworker, James McAllister, she had at least seven siblings and had left school at thirteen years old. Following an affair with Henry Donoghue, she became pregnant and was married on February 19, 1916, when she was only seventeen. She had several pregnancies, and three of her children died soon after childbirth. As sad as this was, her marriage to Henry was far from happy, and they separated in early 1928. Being a single mother in the Glasgow of the late 1920s was an unenviable predicament. She gained some employment as a shop assistant and moved in with her brother on Kent Street in the rough Gorbals District. So, when May received an invitation to go for a night out to a new Italian ice-cream parlor, she was delighted to accept.*

---

* Whether her friend was a man or woman is difficult to ascertain. Mindful that she got married because she was pregnant, not because

On a late Sunday summer's evening in August 1928, during Glasgow's Trades Holidays, May Donoghue took a thirty-minute tram ride and met with her friend at the Wellmeadow Café. It was a modern establishment at the intersection of Lady Lane and High Street in Paisley, a Glasgow suburb known for its shawl making and the design pattern favored by sixties hippies. Its hoarding read "Real Italian Ice Cream Saloon"; this was exotic fare for impecunious Glaswegians like May. The café was owned and operated by Francis Minchella. Christened Francesco Minghella, he was from a long line of Italian confectioners who had long ago become a feature of Scottish life. Although the building was old and had been a popular spot for various eateries, being across from a church and near the centre of Paisley, Francis had only opened his café a year or so earlier. He rented from a local lawyer, named William Reid.

May's friend took charge of proceedings at the café. Just before nine o'clock, as a treat for May, her friend ordered May the Scottish equivalent of an ice-cream float, which consisted of two scoops of ice-cream covered in ginger beer: she had a pear and ice for herself. As was customary, she paid Mr. Minchella for the confections when they were

she was in love, and was now separated, it might have been a man. This would explain why she was willing to trek across town to visit him; she would also have had the benefit of being outside her regular neighborhood to avoid wagging tongues. Even if the companion was female, she might have simply wanted to escape the dismal reality of being destitute, divorced, and a single parent.

Figure 6.1. The Wellmeadow Café (The store sign – in front of the little girl in a white dress – says: "Real Italian Ice Cream Saloon.") (Photo from the Paisley Museum).

served; the dine-and-dash routine was already a common occurrence.

Mr. Minchella served the ice-cream concoction himself. The ginger beer bottle was uncorked by Mr. Minchella, and half of it was poured by him on to May's ice cream. The bottle was made of dark and opaque glass; it was impenetrable to the human eye and, therefore, incapable of intermediate inspection to determine whether there was anything other than ginger beer inside. The reason for this bottling practice was to mask the sediment in the drink caused by the use of yeast, which was used to give the drink its slightly alcoholic kick (below 2 percent proof). May tucked into her ice-cream indulgence and was enjoying her evening out on the town as

Figure 6.2. Stevenson Bottle, which reads "D. Stevenson, Glen Lane, Paisley." Photo Taken by Michael Taylor.

a woman of relative means. When she had consumed much of the float, her friend reached over to refresh her confection by pouring out the remainder of the ginger beer. To both of their dismay, the partly decomposing remains of a snail popped out into her tumbler of ice cream. And that famous mollusk, real or imagined, had made its appearance on the broader legal stage as well as in the Wellmeadow Café.

Exactly what happened next is unclear. According to May, who was generally of a strong constitution, she began to feel ill. The sight of the snail triggered her delayed reaction to consuming the contaminated ginger beer. Things went from bad to worse. Wretching and vomiting, she returned home with the help of her friend. She became so ill that she was unable to go to work the next day. At the time, people like May had no regular doctor or health care. However, as the symptoms persisted, she was forced to take the unusual step three days later of visiting a doctor who diagnosed her with gastroenteritis. Try as she might, she could not shake off her ailments. So debilitated and desperate was she that three weeks later in September, she received emergency treatment at the Glasgow Royal Infirmary. Fortunately, this seemed to work, and she began to recover sufficiently that she was able to resume her job as a shop assistant and much of her normal life. Her night out had turned into almost a month's illness.

Although May's illness was more extreme and lengthy than normally is the case, there was nothing unusual about finding some foreign object in food. Even today, few people have not had the unsettling experience of finding something in a packet of cereal or in an order of salad that was not supposed to be there. Recently, an unfortunate patron at an Ontario McDonald's claimed to find a rat's head in her Big Mac, and a former student found a mouse baked into a loaf of bread that he purchased. These are extreme cases, but their occurrence is far from uncommon. However, what is distinctly unusual in May's case is that she decided not only to begin a legal action but also to take it all the way to the United Kingdom's highest court. Most disgruntled and damaged consumers make an initial fuss and threaten all kinds of redress, but very few actually go as far as instituting legal proceedings; most settle for some 'free lunch' or small financial compensation as the realities of litigation set in. But not Mrs. Donoghue; she was in for the long haul.

In truth though, it is perhaps more down to the determined efforts of her lawyer, Walter Leechman, than May herself. With an office in Glasgow's West George Street, he was a city councillor and had made it his life's cause to champion the neglected rights of the common person. A devoted apiarist and nature lover, he had a reputation as a scrupulous and meticulous lawyer (which suggests that he had checked out and believed May's version of the facts). With tenacity and principled persuasion, he had taken particular aim at the pathetic state of negligence law, particularly as it applied to consumers. As things would have it, he had a definite animus toward ginger-beer manufacturers.

A few years earlier, he had begun to prosecute a series of cases in which mice had turned up in other bottles of ginger beer. The most important of these cases went on appeal, but he was ultimately defeated in a case before the Inner House of the Court of Session: the judgment in this case was ultimately handed down on March 20, 1929. Bloodied but unbowed, Leechman commenced May's claim only twenty days later in April. He was not to be deterred from his self-proclaimed mission to change the law so that manufacturers would owe a duty of care to the ultimate consumers of their products.

It was, of course, May's good fortune that she was befriended by this Don Quixote of the law. He was likely the only lawyer in Glasgow who would take the case of such a penniless litigant, no matter how deserving her claim. It is not entirely clear how the case was financed. By the end of 1929, she had already incurred in excess of £100 (about $200) in legal costs, which would have far exceeded anything that she could afford. It was likely that Leechman took this case either on a contingency basis (being paid only if she won) or for free. However, it is known that May was accorded the status of a person suing *in forma pauperis*, which meant that she would not be liable for Stevenson's cost if she was unsuccessful. There was an affidavit sworn by May in the case that stated "I am very poor" and "am not worth in all the world the sum of Five Pounds"; this was accompanied by a certificate attesting that Mrs. Donoghue was a "very poor person," signed by the minister and elders of her church in Glasgow. In short, unlike so many other deserving but penurious litigants, May's case went forward because of the kindness of strangers, in this case, the crusading Leechman.

It took Leechman little effort to determine that the bottle of ginger beer in question was manufactured by the local David Stevenson Jr., known to family and friends as Davie. His bottling plant was located 650 yards from Minchella's Wellmeadow Café on nearby Glen Lane in Paisley. His family had been in the fizzy-drinks business since the 1870s, and he had a reputation for running his plant operations with a military efficiency. Nevertheless, snails and slugs were not an unusual sight or pest in factories of the time; they were everywhere in the rain-sodden Scottish climate. Moreover, even though Stevenson's name was stamped into the glass, the problem was that Stevenson's bottles were often returned to other brewers, who could utilize them as their own and fill them with their own concoction. The manufacturing processes of many of these plants had very mixed standards of efficiency and cleanliness. Indeed, Stevenson's plant did have something of a good reputation for utilizing sterile processes.

Leechman had his mind made up – he would take May's case. The basis of the claim would have to be negligence. Because it was May's friend who had ordered and bought the ice creams and not May, it was clear that May had no contract that she could sue on. Consequently, it was necessary to frame her legal assertions on the basis that there had been negligence in allowing the ginger beer to be manufactured, sold, and served with a dead and decomposing snail in it. Furthermore, because Francis Minchella had not been negligent, in that he was unable to notice the snail in the bottle even if he had tried to inspect it, the only person to pursue was the manufacturer. So an action was commenced against Stevenson for £500. At the heart of the legal pleadings was the allegation that "slimy trails of snails" were "frequently found" on the manufacturer's premises and that

Stevenson had failed to set up an efficient inspection policy for the bottles so as to ensure that the snails did not find their way into the bottles of ginger beer.

Stevenson was not new to the business of being sued. Nor was he surprised that Walter Leechman was behind the litigation. But he was enraged that his family's good name had been challenged and brought into disrepute by these scurrilous claims. Hiring a prominent firm of Glasgow lawyers, he resolved to fight the case with all means at his disposal. He asserted strenuously in his defense that the bottle in issue was not his and that, even if it were, there was no snail in the bottle; this was a plot by the unscrupulous Leechman to stir up trouble and feather his own nest.

But the initial and ingenious defense of Stevenson was that, even if all the allegations about May's experience and illness were true, they did not reveal a compelling or valid cause of action. Although he denied that they were true, his opening salvo was to seek an order that the pleadings were legally inadequate and to have the case thrown out. He relied on then-recent decisions by the Scottish courts that exonerated food manufacturers generally and ginger-beer makers particularly from such claims. Indeed, with a neat symmetry, Stevenson argued that these precedents were in fact established in cases brought by Leechman himself. Accordingly, the case wended its way through the courts on the basis of a procedural irregularity. It was only once when this preliminary issue was resolved that there would need to be any engagement, if at all, over the facts themselves.

As is so often the case in law, procedure is the handmaiden of justice and, in some cases, injustice.

In 1929, the state of Scottish law was reasonably certain, though certainly not reasonable. The only few occasions on which consumers might bring suit against a manufacturer in circumstances like those of Mrs. Donoghue were when there was a contract between consumer and manufacturer (a rare circumstance in the age of retail stores); the manufacturer knew of the flaw or damage; and the product was an inherently dangerous one, like a car. It was clear that May's claim did not fall into any of these situations. In all other circumstances, the consumer had no right of redress against a manufacturer who could escape scot free, as it were, from injuries or problems that resulted from their products. The most that they might have to do was reimburse retailers, like Minchella, from contract claims by aggrieved consumers: this would be a minimal sum.

Nevertheless, by luck or good argument, in the first court hearing on May 28, 1930, it was declared that a cause of action did exist, as long as the facts alleged by May against Stevenson could be proved. In a forceful decision, the relatively iconoclastic Lord Moncrieff likely relied on the less conservative thrust of American jurisprudence and stated, "I am unhesitatingly of opinion that those who deal with the production of food or produce fluids for beverage purposes ought not be heard to plead ignorance of the active danger

which will be associated with their products, as a consequence of any imperfect observation of cleanliness at any
stage in the course of the process manufacture." However,
this victory was short lived.

A few months later, in the Second Divisions of the Court
of Sessions, the earlier decision was overruled, and it was
held that Mrs. Donoghue had no legal basis for her claim and
that Stevenson was, therefore, not liable for her injuries and
lost wages. Four judges sat on the appeal, and three of them,
Lord Justice Clerk Alness, Lord Ormidale, and Lord Anderson, confirmed that they were bound by their own earlier
decision in the mouse cases brought by Leechman and other
like-minded lawyers. They went out of their way to upbraid
Lord Moncrieff for not following those precedents and for not
dismissing May's claim: "an elaborate Opinion which seems
to show – if this may be said without disrespect – a disincli-
nation on his Lordship's part to acquiesce in the law as it had
been declared, rather than any real misapprehension." In a
bold dissent, the last of the four judges, Lord Hunter, continued his unwillingness to follow the mouse cases, in which
he had also and consistently dissented. He was squarely
of the opinion that May should at least have been granted
the opportunity to go forward and try her case; she should
not be preempted from proceeding on procedural grounds
alone.

Undaunted, Leechman made the final maneuver available to May – he applied for leave to appeal to the Judicial
Committee of the House of Lords, the highest court of appeal

for all cases in the United Kingdom, including Scottish cases. Her petition to appeal *in forma pauperis* was presented on February 26, 1931, and granted on March 17, 1931. All was now set for the final showdown in which there was much more at stake than the commercial relations between ginger-beer manufacturers and their clients.

Leechman, but not May, traveled down to London to listen to arguments in December 1931. As was and remains the custom, local lawyers brief more senior counsel on such occasions. May was represented by George Morton (king's counsel) and W. R. Milligan, who was later to become Scotland's lord advocate. Stevenson was represented by an equally august set of lawyers – W. G. Normand, KC; then solicitor general for Scotland and later a law lord himself; J. L. Clyde, later also lord advocate and then lord president of the Court of Session; and T. Elder Jones. An initial hurdle was the fact that the case was under the jurisdiction of the Scottish courts, which were part of a civilian and more code-based system than the English common law's more organic and freewheeling style of legal argumentation. The panel of five law lords who were selected to hear the appeal comprised two Scotsmen, two Englishmen, and a Welshman. In a cursory finding, the court came to the firm, if fictional, conclusion that "for the purposes of determining this problem the laws of Scotland and of England are the same." This crucial finding has been hotly contested ever since by Scottish lawyers as a matter of both historical accuracy and legal policy.

The now-famous opinions of the law lords were delivered (and actually read out) on May 26, 1932, almost four
years after the summer evening at the Wellmeadow Café.
In a far-from-common practice, all five law lords delivered
extensive reasons for their decision. In a fascinating mix
of alliances, the committee split 3–2 with the two Scotsmen, Lords MacMillan and Thankerton, and the Welshman,
Lord Atkin, finding in May's favor and the two Englishmen, Lords Buckmaster and Tomlin, dissenting and finding against her. Each of the opinions make for interesting
reading. Although there is no formal protocol for determining which count as the Committee's leading judgments, it is
those of Lord Atkin and Lord Buckmaster that have occupied most lawyers' attention. However, the supporting decision of Lord Macmillan is considered by some to be superior
in argument and cogency.

Although a proud Welshman (and one of the lawyers
to draft the Church of Wales' constitution), Baron James
Richard Atkin was an Australian by birth. His Irish father
and his Welsh mother had emigrated to Australia shortly
before their eldest son's birth; he was born in Brisbane,
Australia, and was the oldest of three boys. However, the
family had returned to his mother's home of Meirionnydd in
mid-Wales when his father had an early death. Not surprisingly, he was greatly influenced by the women in his life – his
grandmother, mother, wife, and four daughters. He married
a Lizzie Hemmant, who had been born within twelve days
and a hundred yards of Atkin's own birth. Lord Atkin was

devoted to his large family of four daughters and two sons who were raised in the family home in Aberdovey. After a successful career as a barrister, he was appointed as judge in 1913 at the age of forty-five and elevated to the House of Lords in 1928. Yet he continued to ride the bus around London, as he thought driving was much too dangerous.

By the time May's appeal came around, Lord Atkin had earned a solid reputation for himself as a keen intellect with a desire for justice: he regularly sought to ensure that he put the attainment of justice above rote adherence to the law. Moving easily between the professional and academic worlds, he was a frequent lecturer at law faculties. Indeed, in a speech to King's College, London on October 28, 1931, a mere six weeks before hearing the arguments in May's case, he talked about the close relation between law and morality. In retrospect, some maintain that his speech foretold the fate of May's claim and the future of negligence law. He concluded his speech by stating, "I doubt whether the whole of the law of tort could not be comprised in the golden maxim to do unto your neighbour as you would that he should do unto you." It is this openly biblical theme that splices together his judgment in the appeal.

In a wide-ranging opinion, Lord Atkin took the view that the judge's task was to detect the underlying legal principles of which the case law was merely illustrative: "in English law there must be, and is, some general conception of relations giving rise to a duty of care, of which the particular cases found in the books are but instances." In line with this general sentiment, he analyzed the relevant cases and spotted a thread that was slowly emerging and that animated the continuing development of recent law. In one of the most majestic and most influential statements of legal principle in the common law world, Lord Atkin said:

> The rule that you are to love your neighbour becomes in law, you must not injure your neighbour; and the lawyer's question, Who is my neighbour? receives a restricted reply. You must take reasonable care to avoid acts or omissions which you can reasonably foresee would be likely to injure your neighbour. Who, then, in law is my neighbour? The answer seems to be – persons who are so closely and directly affected by my act that I ought reasonably to have them in contemplation as being so affected when I am directing my mind to the acts or omissions which are called in question.

With this sweeping statement of principle, Lord Atkin set in motion an interpretive process that continues to this day across the legal world. However, the origins of this grand precept are much closer to home. It was Lord Atkin's practice to use his family as a sounding board for his decisions. At the family dining table, he would often tell his children of the cases that he was working on and seek their reaction. One evening, he asked them about May's case. Drawing on their Sunday-school training, they responded by talking about the parable of the Good Samaritan and its emphasis on "love your neighbor." Mulling this over in his chambers later, Lord Atkin worked up this casual reference into what is arguably still the leading judgment in all the common law world. For some, Lord Atkin's way of proceeding was inappropriate and unprofessional, but for others, it leavened the law's high-mindedness with a much-needed dose of common sense.

The main dissenting opinion was delivered by Lord Buckmaster. His father was a self-made man and had been gifted a peerage that passed to Stanley Owen on his death. He first made his name in politics and was appointed solic-itor general, a senior law officer of the government, before he became lord chancellor and leader of the House of Lords. In light of his dissent in the Donoghue case, it was ironic that he had earned a political reputation as a long-standing and enthusiastic Liberal who developed more radical Labour leanings later in life. A renowned orator, he was a supporter of divorce law reform, women's suffrage, birth control, and improved living conditions for the poor, and he was opposed to capital punishment. Yet in his capacity as a judge, he was a traditionalist; he resisted any temptation to correct bad laws and maintained that the remedy in such hard cases was for parliament, not the courts.

In refusing to go with Lord Atkin and the majority, Lord Buckmaster was not inured to the injustice of May's situ-ation. Instead, he insisted that it was his judicial duty to apply existing law, not to bend it to relieve hardship, no matter how compelling. Accordingly, he hewed close to past precedents on the mouse cases and refused to be guided by any overarching or developing principle in the law. Finding against May's claim, he struck a defiant, if alarmist, note that was music to the ears of all those conservatives who warned against the allure of the slippery slope:

> If one step, why not fifty? Yet if a house be, as it sometimes is, negligently built, and in consequence of that negligence the ceiling falls and injures the occupier or anyone else, no action against the builder exists according to the English law, although I believe such a right did exist according to the laws of Babylon.

So after four years, much expense, and legal wrangling, May Donoghue was permitted to bring her case. But nothing more. The House of Lords had merely decided that, if she could establish all the facts on which her claim was based, she would stand to win her case. The law lords remitted her case back to the Court of Sessions in Glasgow for proof of the facts. Accepted by that court on July 19, 1932, a trial date was set for January 10, 1933. This, of course, was a 'big ask.' There were so many evidential barriers to be hurdled before she would be home safe and dry. It was now for May to demonstrate to the court's satisfaction that there indeed had been a decomposed snail in her ginger beer, that the ginger-beer bottle was manufactured by Stevenson, and that this was the cause of her severe bout of gastroenteritis.

But for Leechman, the holy grail of manufacturers' liability in negligence had already been reached. The highest court in the United Kingdom had vindicated his cause and placed a duty to take reasonable care for the safety of their customers. Emboldened by Lord Atkin's opinion, he knew that even Scottish judges (of whom he had a low opinion) would have to sit up and take note. Henceforth, he could be assured that, whatever the fate of May Donoghue's claim, other customers and consumers could begin to rein in the shabby and lackadaisical practices of indifferent manufacturers. His gamble on May had already come home and been paid in full.

The reaction to the law lords' decision in *Donoghue (or M'Alister)* v. *Stevenson*, as it was formally reported, was predictably mixed. But there was more support than criticism. Among the legal community, it was celebrated as a necessary step forward in negligence law and as a decision that brought the law more in line with contemporary sensibilities. Lord Atkin was praised by the eminent Sir Frederick Pollock in the *Law Quarterly Review* for "overriding the scruples of English colleagues who could not emancipate themselves from the pressure of a supposed current of authority in the English Courts." Insofar as it pierced public consciousness, there was warm approval. Whereas the newspaper the *Scotsman* wrote that the decision "should be welcomed by the public," the *Law Times* said that the decision was "revolutionary" and represented a "radical change" in tort law that was "strictly in accord with the needs of modern economic times."

Yet the importance and significance of the case was not automatic and had to be earned over time. "Greatness" was a label that was not stuck to the decision because of its intellectual or legal right but because it gained the approval of the judicial community in later judgments. The appeal of Lord Atkin's opinion was its suggestive and broad language; it pointed in certain directions but left open its precise meaning in particular circumstances. As with the ginger-beer bottle, there was a certain opacity to the judgment. As do great works of literature, it left much to be determined by its later readers. As is Shakespeare's *Hamlet*, Lord Atkin's *Donoghue* opinion is considered great not only because of its profundity but also because of its profligacy. It lends itself to diverse and contestable renderings by opening up rather than closing down interpretive options. In short, it is because of its Delphic or oracular quality, not in spite of it, that the neighbor principle launched on its path to legal greatness.

In many ways, the history of negligence law over the past seventy-five years or so has been a battle between the judicial conservatives and the liberals. In his supporting judgment (and what is considered the swing vote), the recently appointed Lord MacMillan had refused to go as far as Lord Atkin in potentially extending liability to all negligent actors; he had confined himself to the manufacturer-consumer relationship. However, he did throw down the gauntlet to later generations of jurists by declaring that "the categories of negligence are never closed." This stood in sharp contrast to the judicial philosophy of Lord Buckmaster and his cautious "if one step, why not fifty?" approach. The development of legal doctrine has been informed by this tension between what another famous judge, Lord Denning, has termed "bold spirits" and "timorous souls." The focus of judicial engagement has obviously been the precise definition to be given to who counts as legal neighbors, what activities they are responsible for, and which injuries and losses are included.

In May's action, it happened to be the case that she and Stevenson were actual neighbors as well as figurative ones; Stevenson's bottling plant was a few hundred yards from the Wellmeadow Café. However, it is clear that Atkin had a much broader zone of neighborhood in mind in mapping the zone of legal liability. Indeed, it has been the opportunity and onus of subsequent judges and scholars to give that neighborly district some substance and detail. In *Donoghue*, the immediate question before the court was whether a ginger-beer manufacturer could be liable to someone who became ill after drinking some ginger beer with a dead snail in it but who had had the drink bought for them. But Lord Atkin's judgment can be (and has been) not unreasonably interpreted to support a range of rulings that run from those declaring that Scottish manufacturers of opaque bottles of ginger beer are expected to check that dead snails are not left in them to those declaring that all persons who make goods or offer services to the public must ensure that they are fit for their intended purpose, and everyone should act with due care in their interactions with others.

As such, there is no one overriding *ratio* (or strict ruling) that can be drawn from *Donoghue*. Depending on the context in which the inquiry is made, the leading judgment of Lord Atkin can be convincingly and legitimately analyzed to produce a vast array of rulings. Some of those challenges include:

- *What does it tell us about the responsibility of persons for statements as opposed to acts?* The law now recognizes that those who are in the business of giving (e.g., accountants, lawyers, banks) owe a duty to people who seek their advice but in more limited circumstances than those for acts that cause personal injury or property damage.
- *What does it tell us about liability for omissions or failure to act?* The law now recognizes that people may be required to act to rescue other persons with whom they have some preexisting relation but no duty to strangers in general.
- *What does it tell us about recovery for loss of profits?* The law has gone back and forth on whether there is liability for so-called pure economic losses that are brought about by negligent conduct if it is unaccompanied by personal injury or property damage.
- *What does it tell us about the liability of public bodies as opposed to private individuals?* Although the law has extended negligence liability to municipalities and other public bodies, it has closely circumscribed the circumstances in which liability will arise, particularly if it involves harm to the general public.

Although there have been a variety of legislative initiatives, the responsibility for developing and clarifying these issues has been left with the courts. But as the decades have passed, although there is more certainty in some areas, each decision opens up as much debate as it closes down; new answers invite new questions. This is the common law way. Although the judges tend to frame their decisions and reasons in law talk, they are inevitably influenced and affected by the shifting tenor of the times. There may be no direct cause-and-effect relationship between changing political and social values and judge-made law, but there is a general tracking over time. As is everyone else, judges are social actors, and their individual commitments find their way into their work to a greater or lesser extent. And this is as it should be. If the law is to retain its vitality and relevance, it must be constantly on the move; change is its only constant. As an exemplary common law judge, Lord Atkin's legacy was as much about his general method as it was about his actual decision. Perhaps he deserves his reputation as the law's own Good Samaritan.

So what happened to Mrs. Donoghue, David Stevenson, and Francis Minchella? Was there a snail in the bottle? Or was it all a giant hoax? As history would have it, there never was a trial, and there was no official determination as to whether the snail made himself an unwelcome guest at the Wellmeadow Café on that August evening in 1928. Although the trial was set for January 1933, David Stevenson died from appendicitis a few months earlier in November 1932. Whether this was happenstance or divine judgment is unknown. Because his manufacturing business was not yet incorporated as a company, Stevenson was personally liable for any liabilities or debts incurred. A short while later, his estate settled with May Donoghue for the amount of £200, which exceeded by a considerable margin her lost earnings. Although this was a very substantial amount for May (and would have been the equivalent to about the salary of the average professional), it represented only a very small part of Stevenson's net estate of more than £12,500. Stevenson's fizzy drink business continued and was swallowed up by the large British brewery Ind Coope in the 1960s, which went on to produce Graham's Golden Lager.

Francis Minchella lived much longer but without Stevenson's business success. By the time of the law lords' decision, he was already out of business: the Wellmeadow Café had closed in 1931. This likely had as much to do with the economic depression of the time than with the snail or Mrs. Donoghue's legal action. Francis left the ice-cream trade and found work as a laborer with the Roads Department of Paisley Burgh. Nevertheless, he outlived all the other players in the legal drama and died in 1970 at the age of eighty.

As for May, at the time of the House of Lords' decision, she had moved in with her son at a Maitland Street address

Figure 6.3. May Donoghue with two grandchildren (Scottish Council of Law Reporting).

closer to the commercial center of Glasgow. Little is known about the rest of her life. Her life likely improved with her settlement, and she enjoyed the company of her grandchildren over the years. Her divorce proceedings moved at a snail's pace, and the divorce was not finalized until 1945. Sadly, though, near the end of her life, things took another turn for the worse and she died in a mental hospital on March 19, 1958, at the age of fifty-nine. By the time of her death, May chose to be known neither as Donoghue (nor

McAlister, McAllister, or M'Alister) nor as May: she adopted the name Mabel Hannah, her mother's names. She almost certainly went to her grave without knowing or appreciating the massive significance of her night out at the Wellmeadow Café.

There is much to learn about life and law from the snail case. At the top of the list must be the almost-ridiculous and haphazard way in which the common law develops and grows. Reliance on the purely fortuitous series of events that occurred to May Donoghue in Paisley seems such a strange way to achieve a just system of legal rules. There were so many obstacles along the way – such as evidence and financing – that had deterred and prevented others from coming forward. For that reason, we owe a debt of gratitude to the persistence not only of Walter Leechman but also to David Stevenson, both of whom refused to let pragmatic compromise get in the way of what they thought was important moral principle – and of course, to the snail, mythical or otherwise. It remains a highly prized member of the law's menagerie.

7

An Aboriginal Title

The Lie and Law of the Land

It still remains surprisingly common to hear talk about the Old World and the New World. The Old World generally refers to the European countries whose seafarers, in the sixteenth and seventeenth centuries, set out on voyages of discovery across the globe. What they discovered was called the New World and is understood to include the Americas (North and South) and Australasia. Of course, the irony of this is that the so-called New World had been home to many established civilizations for thousands of years before being "discovered" by the Europeans. Subjugated and often exterminated by these invaders, aboriginal nations and communities have only recently begun to seek justice and redress for the historical wrongs done to them.

At the heart of many of these claims is the disputed issue of land ownership. Upon being "discovered," many aboriginal groups were obliged or persuaded to transfer vast tracts of land to their new neighbors. Apart from the freedom of these exchanges, much was complicated by the fact that such groups had a very different understanding about the relationship between people and land than the Europeans. Against this fraught political and historical background, courts have been asked to determine claims by aboriginal people, individually and collectively, as to their rights over traditional lands and to continue traditional activities. None of these cases was as contested or became as notorious as an Australian case that highlighted the opportunities and obstacles of framing such political disputes in legal terms.

There have been people living in Australia for more than forty thousand years. At the end of the eighteenth century, the Australian mainland and Tasmania were inhabited by about 250 separate nations of indigenous people. There was a total population of around five hundred thousand when Europeans made permanent settlements there. Although there was considerable peaceful coexistence, each nation had its own language and proudly guarded its own traditions and culture. However, by 1996, the number of communities had been drastically reduced, few languages thrived, and the population was down to about 280,000 (or about 2 percent of Australia's total population), although since then there has been a steady increase. The living standards, educational facilities, and general plight of aboriginal peoples tend to be very low and they are substantially worse than those for the bulk of the country's nonaboriginal population.

One group of Australian aboriginals is the Torres Strait Islanders. Inhabiting the many small islands between the northern tip of Queensland and Papua New Guinea, they have developed a language and culture that is a unique mix of Australian, Papuan, and Melanesian aboriginal traditions. About six thousand people live on the islands themselves, but the majority of Torres Islanders live in the mainland cities of Townsville and Cairns. Since 1879, almost all of the 274 islands have been part of Australia's Queensland State, which exercises sovereignty over them. The islands have been governed by a variety of semiautonomous regional authorities, but the white community has always dominated to greater or lesser degrees.

Eddie Mabo was a Torres Strait Islander. Although his early years and experience were typical, he became one of a handful of islanders who took a very atypical stand in confronting the personal and institutional discrimination that his people continued to endure. He was born Eddie Koiki Sambo on Mer Island (known, in English, as Murray Island) on June 29, 1936; he was the fifth child of Robert and Poipe Sambo. Sadly, his mother died shortly after his birth, and he was farmed out to his mother's brother, Benny Mabo, and his wife, Maiga. They adopted him and brought him up as their own. In addition to thinking of Benny as his father, Eddie always insisted that he was treated by customary law as being his uncle's legal child, and he carried his name, Mabo.

He grew up in the village of Las, on the northeast corner of Mer, where indigenous tradition and Western influences were delicately intermingled. Under the auspices of Queensland's chief protector of Aborigines and the Department of Native Affairs, Eddie received only basic schooling; it was assumed that no aboriginal child had the ability to benefit from more. However, young Eddie was already singled out by his government-imported teacher, Robert Miles, as a likable and precocious student of real potential. He helped him learn and develop his English.

But Eddie was a rambunctious and impatient young man. When he was sixteen, he was found guilty of drunken and disorderly conduct and had been accused of having an illicit relationship with an island girl. He was sentenced to a year of exile on Thursday Island; this was the administrative headquarters of the Torres Strait and was reserved exclusively for white residents.

At this time, islanders like Eddie were not full citizens of the Australian state; they had no right to vote and needed permission to move around. Rather than being an unpaid garbage collector, Eddie worked on a local pearling lugger for a couple of years before returning to Mer. On his return, he continued for a little while as a dockhand on another lugger. But he knew that the mainland was where the money was. So, in 1957, at twenty years old, he left the security of his family to chance his luck on the mainland.

In 1950s Queensland, life for "blacks" like Eddie was no picnic. Employment was scarce and, even when found,

Figure 7.1. Eddie Koiki Mabo.

poorly paid. Soon after he arrived there, he met his aboriginal wife, Bonita Nehow, or Netta, as he called her. They were married in 1959 and in 1962, with a young family, moved to Townsville, a city of one hundred thousand people or so. Together, they raised seven children of their own and adopted three more from their extended family. In and out of employment, Eddie became involved in aboriginal politics. Apart from carrying a grudge about his own treatment, he was committed to bettering the plight of the Australian aboriginal. He became, as one biographer noted, "a shit-disturber *par excellence.*" Not always popular among his own aboriginal people, he played an activist role in the belated and hard-fought campaign to give aboriginal and islander people the right to vote. It took until 1967 to achieve that basic right. But having made that breakthrough, expectations were raised that further and steady progress could be made.

Although Eddie had spent most of his adult life on the mainland, he missed the islands: he talked frequently about returning there. Over the following ten years or so, he eased his homesickness by becoming part of various islander organizations. But his often-headstrong personality did not always endear him to his fellow islanders. From 1967 to 1975, he worked as a gardener at James Cook University, where he took advantage of the school's library and educated himself further about the history of the islanders. He contributed to courses and seminars on aboriginal history and politics. He became more and more attached to his aboriginal heritage as an intellectual pursuit, a personal project, and a political commitment. He established the Townsville Black Community School, and his involvement gained him national recognition; he was appointed to Australia's Aboriginal Arts Council and the National Aboriginal Education Committee.

Much of Eddie's drive and passion can be traced back to 1973. At that time, he had not been home since 1957.

His father, Benny, was ill, and only one of Eddie's children had met their grandfather. He decided to take his wife and family on a trip to Mer Island. However, when they reached Thursday Island, he received a telegram from the chairman of the Murray Council refusing him permission to come to the island. His father died without Eddie seeing him again. It was only in 1977 that he returned to Mer Island briefly without anyone's permission. At this point, it was Eddie's understanding that he had inherited land from his father. When he was told that the land was Crown land and not his or his family's, Eddie vowed that he would never give up his claim to the land – "it's not theirs, it's ours."

With a deepening sense of grievance and personal hurt, Eddie attended a conference on land rights at James Cook University in 1981. It was to be an event that changed not only Eddie's life but also that of most Australians, whether aboriginal or white. Eddie was invited to participate and spoke powerfully about the islanders' claims to own their own land and the customary regime of property ownership on the Islands. Riding a rising international wave of interest in such matters, several prominent lawyers had attended and were particularly taken by Eddie's talk and his own experience. Greg McIntyre was there. He was a young lawyer at the Aboriginal Legal Service in Cairns. Supported by the Aboriginal Treaty Committee's Doctor "Nugget" Coombs and anthropologist Nonie Sharp, he agreed to act as the solicitor in a possible test case to establish the land rights of the Torres Strait Islanders through the court system. The *Mabo* litigation was primed and ready to launch.

Five men from Mer – Eddie Mabo, Sam Passi, Father Dave Passi, James Rice, and Celuia Mapo Salee – were recruited as plaintiffs. In addition to Greg McIntyre, the legal team would come to consist of Barbara Hocking (who was a Melbourne barrister, a longtime advocate for aboriginal rights, and twisted the arms of others to get involved), Ron Castan (who was one of the country's leading queen's counsels and champion of lost causes), and Bryan Keon-Cohen (a young barrister who served as junior counsel). In an unusual procedure, the case commenced before Australia's highest court, the High Court, in Canberra. Unlike similar institutions in other countries, the High Court not only had appellate jurisdiction but also was obliged under its original jurisdiction to hear some claims directly and from the beginning. It promised to be a case that was almost guaranteed to make significant waves. And it was no disappointment.

The *Mabo* action was brought against the state of Queensland. Although there had been little litigation in Australia, a considerable body of Commonwealth law and jurisprudence had developed around the concept of native title. Although a matter of long-running controversy, the general approach had been that Australia was *terra nullius* (no one's land).

Figure 7.2. The plaintiffs and their legal counsel.

At the end of the eighteenth century, it was treated as uninhabited by the British because there was only a "primitive" form of social organization there. This meant that there was assumed to be no applicable local laws in existence; therefore, the law of England was regnant – all land belonged to the Crown and could be dealt with without any regard to native claims. Consequently, although the Queensland government reserved Murray Island for native inhabitants in 1882, this did not confer any further or special rights on the islanders. English law remained the law of the land, and all property was owned entirely by the Crown without restriction. It was as if the Torres Strait Islands were a physically part of the distant United Kingdom itself.

Eddie and the other plaintiffs based their legal claims on a very different set of arguments and understandings. They contended that Queensland's sovereignty over Mer Island was subject to the land rights of the Torres Strait Islanders based on local custom and traditional title. Although the islanders had been brought under the general sovereignty of Australia, this did not extinguish the aboriginal system of land holdings on Mer. Known as Malo's law, this religiously inspired series of teachings and precepts laid down how islanders should worship and relate to the land; it also provided for essential rules about inheritance from one generation to another. In effect, Eddie and his fellow islanders insisted that, although the land had been stolen, their rights still prevailed and should be recognized. Even though it was claimed that "the only real islander is one who follows Malo's law," a looming issue was that this scheme was based not on documents but on an oral tradition that was difficult to prove in nonaboriginal forums. Malo's law did not seem robust enough to stand up to the English law juggernaut..

Apart from the many legal obstacles to be overcome, there were two major problems for the islanders. First, there was the pressing issue of how to finance the litigation. Suing a conservative Queensland government, they were up against a defendant with the deepest of pockets and with a political mandate to resist any of their claims. Although they struggled throughout, they did receive a grant of $50,000 from the federal government. Nevertheless, Eddie and the others had to draw on their own meager savings to keep the litigation on track; this took its toll in many ways.

Second, the islanders were far from united in their support of Eddie's claim. His uncompromising personal nature and the fact that he had left Mer twenty-five years before and still wanted a say in the political and social life of their island fueled suspicion. Always steep and demanding, the hill of litigation and change looked especially formidable in the early 1980s.

After months of legal and historical research, the plaintiffs' statement of claim was lodged at the Brisbane registry of the High Court of Australia on May 20, 1982. Three months later, the Queensland government sought to strike out the claim as "frivolous and vexatious." Contending that it revealed no reasonable cause of action, the government made a whole array of arguments around native title. In particular, in addition to relying on the heft of legal precedents in their apparent favor, great emphasis was placed on the fact that the island's conversion to Christianity had resulted in the islanders' abandonment of their own purely indigenous traditions. Faced with such evidence, the High Court agreed to an indefinite adjournment so that the parties might agree on a statement of facts. For the next three years, Queensland's lawyers utilized the full range of legal maneuvers and procedural tactics to frustrate the plaintiffs and throw the litigation off course. But Eddie and the lawyers gave no real quarter; they were in it for the long haul.

In a contrived fit of political pique, the Queensland government decided that enough was enough. In 1985, it hastily enacted the Queensland Coast Island Declaratory Act. This was a sweeping piece of legislation that declared that native title had been extinguished on the annexation of the islands in 1879 and that title to the islands was vested in the state of Queensland "freed from all other rights, interests and claims whatsoever." This was a potentially litigation-ending move by the government; the exercise of contemporary power would trump any reliance on the historical record. The only option for the Mabo team was to go back to the High Court and challenge the validity of the act.

Although Australia has a written constitution, it did not (nor does it yet have) an entrenched bill of rights. This meant that there was no obvious constitutional equality argument to be made. So, in arguments before the High Court in mid-March 1988, Eddie's counsel contended under general constitutional doctrine that, where there is an inconsistency between a piece of state legislation and a federal one, the federal legislation must prevail. Accordingly, because the Queensland Act of 1985 offended the federal Racial Discrimination Act of 1975, it must be set aside. Later that December, the High Court agreed, but only by a 4–3 majority. It decided that, although the Queensland Act would effectively extinguish the islanders' native title if unchallenged, it would unfairly infringe their federally established right to own and inherit property. The act was declared invalid. This case became known as *Mabo v. Queensland (No. 1)* and enabled Eddie and the others to proceed with their initial claim.

While the expensive and time-consuming distractions of the litigation in *Mabo (No. 1)* were being resolved, the main claim to establish that the islanders had native title was continuing. In February 1986, Chief Justice Harry Gibbs had decided that the case should be referred to Justice Martin Moynihan of the Supreme Court of Queensland, who would be tasked with deciding on the disputed facts of the matter. These proceedings commenced six months later in October 1986. The evidence submitted about the island's history, custom, and Malo's law was voluminous and lengthy. Eddie Mabo alone spent nine full days being examined and cross-examined; he was constantly interrupted by a slew of evidentiary objections. The main challenge by the government was that Mabo's evidence was all hearsay and, therefore, not admissible. Because evidence of an oral tradition cannot be anything other than hearsay, it was a tiresome process. In February 1987, an impasse was reached, and the case was adjourned. It would be left for the proceedings in *Mabo (No. 1)* to complete their way through the system before anything else of consequence happened.

It was only after a further two years that Justice Moynihan reconvened the hearings in May 1989. In an effort to move things along, the parties agreed that the Court should travel to the Torres Strait; hearings were on Mer and Thursday Islands. The judge referred to this as the Great Northern Expedition. Thirty-four islanders and five anthropological experts gave evidence. The court sat for fifty more days until the hearing was finally concluded on September 6, 1989. The relatively inexperienced Justice Moynihan then faced the formidable task of making sense of the welter of evidence presented and testimony heard, which, together with the submissions from both sides, had generated 3,464 pages of transcript and more than 330 exhibits. Eddie Mabo spent the intervening time with his family back in Townsville and worked on his boat, which his neighbors nicknamed Noah's Ark.

More than a year later, on November 16, 1990, Justice Moynihan submitted his report to the High Court. It covered four hundred pages over three volumes. But the conclusions and overall tenor of the judge's findings were a dramatic and painful blow to Eddie and his legal team. Although the judge did confirm that the Mer Islanders had a strong sense of their customary relation to the land and followed its imperatives, he discredited most of Eddie's evidence. He concluded that it was not possible to accept that Eddie had been adopted by his uncle: Eddie was not shown to be entitled to his claimed heritage. Initially gutted by this public denunciation, Eddie managed to recover himself with the support of family and friends. His single-minded determination had been bruised, but it had not been broken. After consulting with his lawyers, it was decided that they should go for broke – they forewent any appeal of Justice Moynihan's findings and, instead, proceeded directly to the final hearing before the High Court.

Eddie made the thirty-six-hour bus ride from Townsville to Canberra in late May 1991. The arguments were more restrained and dignified than some of the earlier encounters between Eddie's counsel and the Queensland lawyers, but the basic hostility was not far below the surface; legal niceties masked a fierce political contest. The presentations lasted three days, and as was their custom, the seven judges retired to reach and write their judgments. There was little left for Eddie and everyone else to do but wait. Eddie returned to Townsville; he worked some more on his boat and enrolled in a couple of further education classes. It took more than twelve months for the High Court to release its decision.

On June 3, 1992, the High Court brought to a close one of the most hotly contested and important cases in its ninety-year history. By a majority of 6–1, the Court held that the fictional concept of *terra nullius* did not apply: Australia's indigenous peoples owned traditional land under native title and that, unless properly extinguished by the Crown, such title retained its legal validity to the present day. This was a historic finding by the High Court and established a general framework for understanding land claims that, in large part, vindicated the long campaign of Eddie Mabo and the islanders. In particular, the High Court held that, although Mer Island was clearly under Australian sovereignty, its land was not Crown land and the Mer Islanders were entitled to possess, occupy, use, and enjoy that land under their customary scheme of ownership and inheritance. It was for the Mer Islanders to decide on Eddie Mabo's claims to his family lands, not the government of Queensland or Justice Moynihan.

But as is so often the case when it comes to judicial decisions, the devil is in the details. Although the judges' general thrust was in the aboriginals' favor, the precise scope and import of the Court's judgments were much more nuanced and debatable. Although the judges were especially concerned with emphasizing that they were offering legal views, not giving political opinions, they stated that "the nation as a whole must remain diminished unless and until there is an acknowledgment of, and retreat from, those past injustices." Unfortunately, the majority of six were divided on their reasons for recognizing native title; they gave four separate judgments. No doubt, the delay in rendering their judgments was in part because of their failed efforts to produce a more united front. All six judges in the majority – Chief Justice Anthony Mason, and Justices Gerard Brennan, William Deane, John Toohey, Mary Gaudron, and Michael McHugh – agreed that native title exists and is recognized by the common law of Australia. However, they disagreed over the conditions under which state governments could extinguish that title and whether compensation had to be paid to aboriginal groups on extinguishment.

The dissenting judgment was given by Justice Daryl Dawson, a former politician and solicitor general of Victoria. He went out of his way to insist that "it would be wrong to attempt to revise history or to fail to recognize its legal impact, however unpalatable it may now seem ... [and] to do so would be to impugn the foundations of the very legal system under which this case must be decided." As did the majority, he also acknowledged the conceptual possibility of native title under Australian common law. However, Dawson came to the firm conclusion that, on annexation of the islands at the end of the eighteenth century, the Crown had assumed ownership and it was unencumbered by any native interests or title.

The ten-year battle had been won, but the centuries-old war between the aboriginals and the state governments continued. *Mabo (No. 2)* had been a significant victory, especially if one considers how debilitating it would have been to the aboriginal cause if it had been lost. Aboriginal groups in other countries set great store by this Australian triumph; it galvanized further their own efforts to advance the push for greater recognition of native land claims. Nevertheless, there was still much to be done if the legal success in the *Mabo* cases was to be turned into positive gains on the ground for aboriginal peoples.

The High Court's ruling in *Mabo (No. 2)* left much undecided. Compared to the protracted court proceedings, the federal government moved quickly to enact the Native Title Act the following year in 1993. The act spoke to two of the most pressing issues that remained. The first was clarifying the framework in which indigenous people were to establish their specific claims to native title. As an alternative to the decade-long and expensive process of *Mabo*-like litigation, the National Native Title Tribunal was created to expedite and streamline the claims process. This did not remove the need for some litigation. But in the ten years after *Mabo*, there were twenty-three agreements reached about native title in different parts of Australia between the parties, and a further seven determinations were made after trials in the federal court.

The second issue was the controversial and crucial matter of fixing the precise ways in which native title can be extinguished. The fact was that the *Mabo* decision would apply only to a small proportion of the aboriginal and Torres Strait Islander population. Any claims to native title on vast tracts of land had long been extinguished; there was nothing in the High Court decision that reversed past extinguishment or revived lapsed claims of native title. However, in a positive move, the 1993 act indicates that native title can be extinguished henceforth only if governments are prepared to pay fair compensation to the holders of native land. There is also a responsibility for the government to consult fully with native title holders before their title can be extinguished. Moreover, the legislation regulates future activities over land where native title exists. In 1995, the federal parliament passed legislation to set up the Land Fund and the Indigenous Land Corporation intended to help indigenous peoples to acquire and manage land.

In spite of these legislative initiatives, aboriginal peoples still took their land claims to the courts. In December 1996, another Queensland case, *The Wik Peoples*, was decided by the High Court; this was the "*Mabo* of the mainland." The Wik inhabited the northern Cape Horn region, and the case concerned whether the government's grant of statutory pastoral leases extinguished their native title rights. This issue had huge implications for Australia in general, as about 50 percent of Australia's total area and 75 percent of land designated for private use was held under such tenure. In a classic confrontation, traditional aboriginal usage was pitted against the mining industry's wish to exploit the land's vast natural resources. In a pragmatic decision, the High Court held in a 4–3 decision that native title was not, as a matter of legal necessity, automatically extinguished by the grant of such pastoral leases: native title rights could coexist with such lease holdings. However, when these rights conflicted, it was the leases that would prevail – native rights to perform ceremonies or gather foods would be extinguished. This decision took some of the luster off *Mabo*, but it did confirm that, at a minimum, native rights held important, if expendable, legal sway.

Of course, the saga of native land claims is not a peculiarly Australian phenomenon. Apart from those nations that simply exterminated the indigenous population on arrival, most of the so-called New World countries face these challenging contemporary dilemmas. Although there are some very important differences, the general path and pattern of political and legal engagement over native land claims has proceeded to similar outcomes. The key issues remain those of establishing the original rights and of deciding when those rights have been extinguished. In doing so, the courts have revealed, despite their efforts to hide the fact, how law and policy are on very intimate terms in such controversial matters.

For instance, in Canada, the repatriation of the Constitution in 1982 led to the inclusion of a provision that stated that "the existing aboriginal and treaty rights of the aboriginal peoples of Canada are hereby recognized and affirmed." The challenge, of course, was for the courts to determine what *existing* and *recognized* meant. Although the courts' jurisprudence is far from reassuringly uniform (or uniformly reassuring), it has tended to take aboriginal rights very seriously. In determining which aboriginal rights are existing, the onus is on the government to demonstrate that there has been a clear extinguishment of any long-held and practiced traditional aboriginal right, including claims to native title. However, the courts have reined in the potential absoluteness of these aboriginal rights by grafting on a rider that recognizes that the federal government retains the general power to impose reasonable restrictions on the exercise of such aboriginal rights. Also, Canadian courts have been prepared to countenance a much more expansive notion of coexistence of aboriginal and nonaboriginal land uses than the Australian courts. Even if there is legal inconsistency, the aboriginal right to use the land can still prevail until the landowner uses the land in a way that is actually inconsistent with the aboriginal rights in issue.

In the United States, the situation is similar to that in Australia, but the courts entered the fray much sooner. Since the *Fletcher v. Peck* decision of 1810, American courts have offered protection to aboriginal claims of native title. Any government grants of land to nonaboriginals, whether made before or after the United States became an independent nation, are considered to exclude native lands or to make them subject to native rights. This means that aboriginal groups retain a right to traditional occupancy, even if they do not retain ownership of the land. Nonetheless, the U.S. Congress retains the absolute right to extinguish native title. Chief Justice Marshall's opinion in 1823 remains valid; "whether it be done by treaty, by the sword, by purchase, by the exercise of complete dominion adverse to the right of occupancy, or otherwise, its justice is not open to inquiry in the courts." However, the federal courts will recognize the effective exercise of such a legislative extinguishment only in the most compelling and clear of circumstances; this has a relatively rare occurrence.

Across the globe, therefore, there seems to be a similar disturbing pattern around the development of native rights. First, aboriginal peoples get very little unless and until they are prepared to fight for it. As did Eddie Mabo, they must demonstrate a heightened commitment and a plucky tenacity to push on in the face of strong odds against them. Second, the courts are prepared to champion native rights to engage in traditional methods of subsistence; they are very reluctant to extend or update those rights so that they can sustain more contemporary modes of economic production or communal existence. And third, legal claims to native title will fare much better when they relate to lands that are not already in nonaboriginal hands or that have little immediate potential for resource development. In short, courts have a bad habit of being fair-weather friends to aboriginal peoples; their support tends to be conditional and partial.

The silver cloud of the *Mabo* litigation had its own dark lining. After the initial hearings before the High Court in May 1991, Eddie Mabo had gone back to his Queensland home in Townsville. But after a couple of months, he began to feel severe pain in his back and chest. By November, he had lost his voice and he could only speak in a hoarse whisper. He was diagnosed with advanced cancer of the throat; a secondary cancer had also spread to his spine. At the age of fifty-five, he was told that his illness was inoperable and that he only had a few months to live. Eddie Mabo died on January 21, 1992. He had missed the final decision in his favor by the High Court of Australia by a mere five months. It was a loss that was tragic in both its occurrence and its timing. But Eddie Mabo has assured for himself a place in history.

Despite his wish to be buried back on Mer Island in his hometown of Las, Eddie was buried in Townsville Cemetery

Figure 7.3. Eddie Mabo's tombstone with Bonita and family members.

on February 1, 1992. His funeral was attended by large num-
bers of people, both dignitaries and ordinary folk, from all
over Australia. After a traditional mourning period of three
years, a later memorial service was held. However, a night
or so later, Eddie's grave site was desecrated by vandals
who spray-painted it with eight red swastikas and daubed
the racist epithet *Abo* on his tombstone; a bronze bas-relief
engraving of him was also removed. This prompted swift
action – his body was transferred to Mer Island. At the

reburial, the islanders performed a traditional ceremony that was reserved for dead kings and that had not been performed for more than eighty years. Eddie would have been delighted by this as much as the many posthumous awards that were bestowed on him. But he would likely have been especially pleased by the fact that on May 21, 2008, James Cook University named its Townsville campus library the Eddie Koiki Mabo Library, after their remarkable gardener.

8

Grinding at the Mill

Putting Limits on Agreements

People make agreements every day; they are ubiquitous and unremarkable. Almost all the time, these agreements go off without a hitch – we shop, we meet friends, we buy coffee, and we travel on public transport. Each involves an arrangement whereby two persons make a commitment to do something together that is usually to the mutual benefit of each. This often but not always involves the exchange of money or services. When problems do arise, people tend to resolve them by some form of negotiation, or they simply lump it. However, there are situations when there is sufficient at stake that people turn to the law for relief or vindication. It is the law's job to decide which agreements it is prepared to treat as giving rise to legal relations and what remedies might be available to an aggrieved party.

Although there are various areas of special rules (e.g., insurance, investment, real estate), the general law of contract lays out the basic framework within which agreement making is regulated. As does the good guest, the law steps in only when invited to do so; there is no general monitoring role whereby the legal process approves or supervises all agreements. But when and where the law is brought into action, its principles and standards evaluate agreements; their performance; and in particular, the consequences of any breach of their express or implied terms and conditions. One issue that goes to the heart of contract law and still occupies the attention of judges and jurists is the calculation of damages that can be claimed if there is a breakdown in legal agreements reached. A relatively old English case still stands as the main origin for the modern law of contract damages.

In mid-nineteenth-century England, the Industrial Revolution was in full flow. The move away from an agrarian-grounded society and community to a more manufacturing-based economy and culture had begun in the late 1700s but had started to gather steam and establish itself across the country by the 1830s and 1840s. The mechanization of textile production, the mining of coal, and the invention of iron-making processes all contributed to this period of immense social change. The expansion in trade led to a massive rise in population, increased migration to urban centers, and the development of a transport infrastructure. All this was accompanied by a vast increase in wealth and opportunities. Whether it was for good or bad depended on where you landed in the social upheaval. As its chronicler Charles Dickens was wont to say about a different revolution, "It was the best of times and the worst of times; . . . it was the spring of hope, it was the winter of despair."

Situated in the southwest of England and close to the Welsh border, Gloucester is a middle-class provincial town that straddles the river Severn. It is almost fifty miles from Birmingham, the nearest of England's many industrial centers, and considered the nineteenth century's workshop of the world. However, in the 1850s, the town of Gloucester had managed to take advantage of the epochal changes in the country and to gain its own special place in the new Industrial Age. It became an unlikely port and gave the landlocked Birmingham access to the wider world of raw materials and global markets.

England's canal network was a technological wonder. Before the advent of the railways, it offered a more economical and effective means to transport bulky materials, like coal and iron ore, across country than by road. In the quarter century from 1791 to 1827, the Gloucester and Sharpness Canal (originally called the Gloucester and Berkeley Canal) was constructed. It ran sixteen miles from Gloucester's docks to the Severn Estuary; this allowed larger seabound ships to go much further up the river than was possible by tidal currents alone. On its completion, it was the longest and widest canal in the country. Providing convenient access to the industrial midlands, the canal gave an unparalleled boost to Gloucester's importance as a maritime center. With the repeal of the Corn Laws in 1846 (which ended import tariffs on corn and other crops), Gloucester began to emerge as the commercial hub of the southwest .

To capitalize on these developments, two local merchants saw their main chance. The Hadley brothers, Joseph and Jonah, decided to build a mill directly at the Gloucester docks; all the existing mills were situated away from the docks and required the further transportation of incoming supplies. Finished in 1850, this state-of-the-art flour mill became known as City Mills and was located in the northern part of Gloucester near Commercial Road. Initially consisting of one building with an adjoining engine house, it was an immensely profitable operation in cleaning and grinding the imported corn. More and better machinery was installed to double the size and capacity of the mill to cope with its commercial success. As part of its commitment to constructing a state-of-the-art facility, the machinery was powered by steam. However, because this technology was still in its relative infancy, the main components were specially designed and custom produced for individual customers; mass production was not yet a staple feature of engineering works.

On Wednesday, May 11, 1853, the Hadleys' steam engine stopped working. The next day, it was established that the breakdown was a result of there being a significant fracture

Figure 8.1. City Flour Mills in the 1920s (Conway-Jones 248).

in the crank of the gear shaft. On Friday, it was reluctantly decided that it would be necessary to return the shaft to the engineers who designed and manufactured it; there were no local outfits up to the task. The manufacturer was Joyce and Co., which was located in Greenwich, near London, more than 125 miles away. The idea was that the broken crankshaft could be used as the pattern for a new shaft which would expedite its production. Needless to say, this was an unwelcome development for the Hadley Brothers. City Mills would be out of service for a while, and substantial profits would be lost as well as further expense incurred.

The Hadleys dispatched one of their office employees to make arrangements for the transporting of the crankshaft to Joyce and Co. He went to the office of Pickford and Co. The firm was owned by Joseph Baxendale. He was the very embodiment of the Victorian entrepreneur par excellence. The son of a successful Lancashire surgeon, he moved to London in 1806 at the age of twenty-one and started working for a wholesale linen draper. While there, he acquired the accounting and managerial skills that would hold him in great stead later in his career. Accumulating a small amount of capital and adding to it substantially with a convenient marriage to a cotton mill owner's daughter, he became a partner in M. Pickford and Co., along with Zachary Langton, Charles Inman, and Hugh Hornby Burley. At this time, it was a floundering carrier in south Manchester; it had been begun as long ago as 1646 by a Will Pickford after the Civil War. But the rise of a truly national economy and burgeoning railway system proved to be everything that the firm needed to recover. By dint of hard work and heartless management, Baxendale made a major contribution to the firm's rise to great profitability and became its managing partner in 1824; he was also heavily involved in the rise of the railways companies.

At the Pickford offices on that Friday morning (Friday the thirteenth), the Hadleys' employee was greeted by a fellow clerk, a Mr. Perret. Exactly what happened in their brief exchange is unclear, but the precise nature of their exchange was of considerable legal importance. One thing is clear – Perret said that, if the crankshaft was delivered to him by twelve o'clock on the next day, it would arrive

Figure 8.2. Joseph Baxendale (Fishman 251).

in Greenwich by rail the following day, Sunday. However, Hadleys' employee claimed that he had told Mr. Perret that the mill was stopped and that it would remain so until the new shaft was installed. Accordingly, he emphasized that the shaft must be sent immediately, and this should be made clear to the actual carriers to hasten its delivery. However, Mr. Perret had no recollection of such an exchange. He maintained that all he was told was that the Hadleys were millers and that the article to be carried was a broken shaft. The resolution of this discrepancy would prove vital in the disposition of the subsequent legal case.

On May 14, a Saturday, the broken crankshaft was delivered to Pickford at eleven o'clock as promised. The amount of £2 and 4 shillings was paid for its carriage. Little else is known about whether there was any exchange of documents or on what particular terms and conditions the agreement of carriage was made. On Sunday morning, a day later, the shaft arrived in London. However, the receiving employees were unaware that the shaft was to be delivered immediately. The shaft did not arrive at Joyce and Co. for a further five days, until May 21, the following Saturday. Meanwhile, City Mills remained idle. Although the Hadleys were expecting a lengthy delay, they did not feel that they should have to carry further the extra losses brought about by the unnecessary delay to its transportation. Pickford denied that it should bear such costs. Accordingly, the circumstances were in place for a legal action – though none of the participants could have anticipated that their relatively minor commercial dispute would become one of the law's most enduring precedents.

In short order, the Hadley brothers had brought their actions against Pickford. In strict legal terms, this was an action brought against Joseph Baxendale personally as the firm's managing partner in the London head office. Partners were personally liable to an unlimited amount for a company's misfeasance. At this time, the proposed move toward the limited and impersonal liability of companies was a hot political issue. It did not become available until a few years later in 1855. So the Hadleys sued Baxendale (hence the name of the case) for £300 in lost profits, although at trial the amount claimed was reduced to a more modest £125. The basis of the Hadleys' claim was that Pickford had been negligent and had failed to fulfill its obligations in a reasonable time. Baxendale admitted that there had been negligence but insisted that the damages claimed were too unforeseeable to warrant compensation. Nevertheless, he paid £25 into court by way of a settlement offer.

The case came on for trial in August 1853, only three months after the incident; this was an expeditious occurrence by any standards. It was heard at the Crown Court at Gloucester's summer assizes before a twelve-person jury of whom nine were local businessmen and the other three property owners; there was likely some sympathy to the Hadleys' plight, as most entrepreneurs had suffered at the hands of careless carriers. The presiding judge was the competent Sir Roger Compton. The prevailing law was that such matters were entirely within the exclusive power of the jury to make an assessment of reasonable damages on the evidence offered. After a very brief trial of a few hours, a compromise verdict was reached in thirty minutes in the Hadleys' favor. Eleven of the twelve jurors agreed to put the losses at £45; the holdout juror would have awarded £75. It was ultimately agreed to set the damages at £50. As Baxendale had already agreed to pay £25, an award of a further £25 was ordered.

Baxendale appealed the decision in November 1853 to the appellate branch of the Exchequer Court. Arguments were heard on February 1 and 2, 1854 by Barons Alderson, Parke, Platt, and Martin. The Hadleys relied on very able London lawyers, being led by Sir Henry Singer Keating, but the prominent Baxendale brought in the big guns; there was much at stake for him and the ambitious Pickfords. His lead counsel was Sir James Shaw Willes, an Irishman from Cork. As was not unusual at the time, he had no formal legal training, but he was an erudite and cosmopolitan man. He was fluent in several languages and had a broad knowledge of foreign legal systems; he is reputed to have defended himself on a murder charge in Spain without the assistance of local counsel. In argument before the Exchequer Court, he urged the judges to look to the wisdom of the French Civil Code and Robert Pothier's celebrated commentary in formulating their decision; a broad rule of recovery would stifle trade and be inexact in operation. Something of a workaholic, he went on to become a judge of the court of common pleas in 1855 and was then appointed to the Privy Council in 1871. But he suffered from poor health in later life and committed suicide on October 2, 1872.

The only issue before the court was the award of damages to the Hadley brothers. The decision of the Court was handed down a few weeks later, on February 23, 1854. In a unanimous judgment, the Court held that Baxendale had prevailed in his appeal and that there should be a new trial so the jury could quantify a precise amount. There is no record of a new trial. It can be assumed only that, having established a ruling that was highly favorable to his transportation firm, Baxendale agreed to settle for an amount at somewhere around £25. And the Hadleys would have accepted; something was better than nothing.

The judgment of the Court was delivered by the sixty-seven-year old Baron Sir Edward Hall Alderson. Coming to the end of his illustrious career, he had been a prodigious student who had excelled in mathematics and classics; he also enjoyed writing Greek odes in his spare time. He was appointed to a judicial position in 1830 and became a baron of the Court of Exchequer in 1834. He forged a strong reputation as a judge who emphasized the need for the common law to be flexible in adapting itself to the changing needs and values of the times. Although often touted as future lord chancellor, he preferred to put his energies off the bench into advancing the cause of High Anglicans in the internecine struggles of the Church of England.

For a judgment of such importance, it was decidedly succinct and, some would add, cut from whole cloth. No academic authors were referenced, and no legal precedents were cited. In ordering a new trial, Baron Alderson stressed the need to provide clear and explicit instruction to the jury. Indeed, the prime motivation of hearing the appeal in the first place and in formulating the judgment was to make awards of damages more predictable: the judges were more

than ready to ride herd over what they saw as increasingly
rogue juries. Consequently, they were as keen to check the
jury's unfettered discretion as they were to impose any particular standard of damage assessment. In its entirety, the
judgment read:

> Where two parties have made a contract which one of them
> has broken, the damages which the other party ought to
> receive in respect of such breach of contract should be such
> as may fairly and reasonably be considered either arising
> naturally, i.e., according to the usual course of things, from
> such breach of contract itself, or such as may reasonably be
> supposed to have been in the contemplation of both parties,
> at the time they made the contract, as the probable result
> of the breach of it. Now, if the special circumstances under
> which the contract was actually made were communicated
> by the plaintiffs to the defendants, and thus known to both
> parties, the damages resulting from the breach of such a
> contract, which they would reasonably contemplate, would
> be the amount of injury which would ordinarily follow from
> a breach of contract under these special circumstances so
> known and communicated. But, on the other hand, if these
> special circumstances were wholly unknown to the party
> breaking the contract, he, at the most, could only be sup-
> posed to have had in his contemplation the amount of injury
> which would arise generally, and in the great multitude
> of cases not affected by any special circumstances, from
> such a breach of contract. For such loss would neither
> have flowed naturally from the breach of this contract in

the great multitude of such cases occurring under ordinary circumstances, nor were the special circumstances, which, perhaps, would have made it a reasonable and natural consequence of such breach of contract, communicated to or known by the defendants.

In short, Baron Alderson had taken the advice of Willes and set up a scheme that was similar to the one in French law. Henceforth, there were to be two separate but related rules in calculating damages for a breach of contract. First, as a general rule, damages should be limited to those that can be assessed as naturally or normally occurring without any special knowledge of events peculiar to the transaction. Second, any damages that might be otherwise considered too remote are recoverable only when they can be anticipated on the basis of special information conveyed at the time of contracting and that could be contemplated only with such detailed knowledge.

So, for example, if we agree that I will drive you to a meeting for a fee, you will be able to claim reasonable damages that occurred for my failure to show up or for getting you lost and missing the meeting; these might include the difference in price between the taxi cab or the bus fare and the predetermined fee, any lost hourly wages, and so on. But you will not be able to claim against me for losing a job if the missed meeting was in fact a job interview, unless you can prove that I knew this and agreed to be responsible for such losses. Of course, in light of the *Hadley* rule, contracting parties will be much clearer about what they do and do not accept in special situations or circumstances.

As regards the Hadleys' claim itself, this meant that much depended on what was and was not communicated between the two clerks on the Friday when the contract between the Hadleys and Baxendale was made. The trial note and headnote of the law report takes Hadleys' line and suggests that the urgency of the situation was conveyed to Pickfords' clerk, Mr. Perret. However, Baron Alderson was adamant that "these special circumstances were never communicated" and that "the only circumstances here communicated by the plaintiffs to the defendants at the time the contract was made, were, that the article to be carried was the broken shaft of a mill, and the plaintiffs were millers of that mill." Furthermore, he maintained that, as it was customary for mills to have a spare shaft, the Hadleys were the partial authors of their own misfortune. Accordingly, although there seems no evidence to support Baron Alderson's view, his finding was decisive and meant that the Hadleys could not avail themselves of the new rule and recover their lost profits.

Despite the fact that Baron Alderson's precise ruling in *Hadley* seemed to come out of the blue, this is far from the case. There were a host of reasons he and his colleagues would have settled on the particular rule that they did. Some of these are reasoned and appealing (even if they will not persuade everyone), but some are of a very dubious provenance.

As suggested already, the judges were concerned with injecting more certainty into the law. This meant that they had to wrest control of damage awards away from the almost-exclusive discretion of juries. There had been a disturbing trend of unpredictable and extravagant awards being made by juries that often favored their local merchants over national concerns. By structuring that discretion in accordance with the *Hadley* rule, they went a long way toward achieving that goal; the rule would shut the floodgates of liability. Henceforth, judges would be able to instruct juries that any award of damages in contractual disputes must conform with the limiting wisdom of the remoteness rule.

The remoteness rule developed by the judges had and continues to have a certain academic pedigree. Under the tutelage of Baxendale's counsel, James Willes, the court had been introduced to the ideas of the French jurist Robert Pothier. In his then-recently-translated *A Treatise on the Law of Obligations*, he had noted that, "when the debtor cannot be charged with any fraud, and is merely in fault for not performing his obligation, . . . the debtor is only liable for the damages and interest which might have been contemplated at the time of the contract; for to such alone the debtor can be considered as having intended to submit." This civilian solution had been cited approvingly in an influential American text, Theodore Sedgwick's *A Treatise on the Measure of Damages*, which had come out in a new second edition in 1852. After the *Hadley* decision, an important factor in ensuring that Baron Alderson's judgment was broadly disseminated and given a scholarly thumbs-up was that counsel Willes was the coeditor (along with, as it happens, Hadley's counsel, Sir Henry Keating) of the most prominent volume of annotated English legal cases at the time, *Smith's Leading Cases*. Baron Alderson's judgment was included in the next edition in 1856. Also, when Willes became a judge, he regularly relied on the judgment in his own decisions.

Indeed, whatever the original academic support for the decision, modern commentators have approved the *Hadley* rule because it reaches an appropriate balance between the plaintiffs' obvious reliance on the defendant and the need to protect the defendant from surprise. Although defendants should be required to provide fair compensation for losses that resulted from their own failure to perform the contract properly or fully, they should not be burdened by having to carry all the unexpected and remote damages that might occur. In the modern parlance of economics, the rule puts the risk on the party who is better placed to protect against the specific consequences that might occur. This usually means that the plaintiff (or defendant) is more able to assess the likely losses and obtain suitable insurance. If the plaintiff chooses not to do so, then it will be their own decision and, therefore, their loss to be carried.

Nevertheless, whatever the intrinsic merits of the *Hadley* decision, it did not assume its status as a leading case without the welcoming reception of the legal and commercial community. Pickford was a national carrier involved in the promotion of the transportation industry whose success was considered essential to the growth and prosperity of the English whole economy. Placing almost-unlimited liability on this fledgling sector would likely have impeded rather than encouraged such important initiatives. As things stood, the cost of transport was relatively low; the Hadleys had paid only slightly more than £2. If Pickford had been liable for damages of £300 in lost profits (or 150 times the initial cost) for the transport of a shaft that itself was valued at only £10, this would have had a very chilling effect on the availability and cost of transport. No transport company would run the risk of such ruinous losses for such small consideration and as a result of such minor contract breaches. The *Hadley* decision was a calculated boost for national entrepreneurs and transport companies.

Of course, this reliance on scholarly work was not driven by any particular regard for academic opinion generally but because it suited the broader agenda of the judges and government. Recent legislation was taking a strong stand in favor of carriers. The Common Carriers Act of 1830 had required that shippers of "articles of great value in small compass" had to declare the value of the shipment; if notice of value was not given, the right to recovery was limited to £10. Interestingly, Baron James Parke, one of the appeal judges in *Hadley*, had been one of the key supporters of that act. Even though the shaft was not of small compass,

it seemed to fall within the natural spirit of that enactment. Furthermore, Parliament was about to make various
reforms to the 1830 act that would further limit the liability
of common carriers. Those legislative changes were made in
April 1854, only two months after the *Hadley* decision. In a
certain sense, the judges of the Exchequer Court had simply brought the anticipated changes into effect a few weeks
earlier.

However, along with these academic and political explanations for the decision, there may well have been less
proper and more personal forces at work. Two of the four
judges in *Hadley* had personal connections with Pickford
and Co. The most intimate was that Baron Parke's brother
was actually Baxendale's predecessor as Pickford's managing director. Also, Baron Samuel Martin had been retained
for many years by Baxendale as Pickford's standing counsel before he became a judge. In an earlier contracts case,
he had represented Baxendale seven years before *Hadley*
in 1847 (and on which both Barons Alderson and Parke
were judges). He had argued strenuously that Pickford, as
a carrier, should be liable only for those expenses of which
it had direct notice and that were of reasonable scope. In
light of these connections, it comes as little surprise that
Parke and Martin were well-disposed toward carriers generally and Pickford in particular. Admittedly, neither judge
gave an opinion in *Hadley*, but they did join in Baron Alderson's judgment. Although such connections might now be

expected to require that judges recuse themselves from hearing and deciding such cases, lest the decision be rendered invalid, there seemed to be no such compunction in the mid-nineteenth century.

Hadley v. Baxendale remains the fountainhead for all common law discussion about the test for the award of damages in contracts cases. It has become known as the foreseeability rule, even though there is no mention of the word *foreseeability* in Baron Alderson's judgment – consequential damage can be recovered only if, at the time the contract was made, the breaching party had reason to foresee that the consequential damages would be the probable result of the breach. This rule soon became part of the common law systems across the globe and remains dominant today. This occurred more as a result of its obvious substantive appeal than because of any reliance on precedential authority (because it did not have much) or by virtue of its compelling argumentation (because it did not have any).

As expected, the decision in *Hadley* builds on several principles that had already been established and would be further refined over the years by the courts:

* *To Be Expected* – It had been determined in an earlier decision, with Baron Parke as the judge, that the general basis for awarding damages in contract cases was

that of expectation. It was held that, "where a party sustains a loss by reason of a breach of contract, he is, so far as money can do it, to be placed in the same situation, with respect to damages, as if the contract had been performed." This meant that, unlike tort law (see Chapter 6), the measure of damage was forward looking (i.e., what would have happened if all went well) as opposed to backward looking (i.e., what the situation was before the wrong).

- *A Liquid Approach* – The *Hadley* rule was called into action only when the parties to the contract had not stipulated the damages to be paid on various breaches. Although there is no requirement to do so, the parties can stipulate damages in the contract; these are known as liquidated damages. However, they must represent a genuine attempt to preestimate damages; a penalty clause that imposes unreasonable damages is not enforceable.

- *A Matter of Performance* – The law of contracts is generally indifferent as to whether a contractual promise is performed or to whether a party pays compensation for not performing. Although ordering full performance of the contract would naturally seem like the purest form of expectation recovery, the courts have been very reluctant to order specific performance. It is only when plaintiffs have demonstrated that damages are not available or will be completely inadequate that the courts will do so. So, specific performance might be ordered for the sale of a unique piece of property with no substitute in the market (e.g., land with a special view, an antique heirloom). Practically speaking, it is considered simply more efficient to award damages, and there is no need for continuing judicial supervision. Concerns of involuntary servitude arise when contracts for personal services (e.g., actors, singers) are specifically enforced. European civilian law takes a very different approach.

- *Mitigating circumstances* – All plaintiffs are required to take reasonable steps to keep their losses as low as practically possible; they must not incur unreasonable expenses. So when a store refuses to accept delivery of perishable goods, the supplier cannot simply let the goods rot; they must try to resell them. In the event that plaintiffs fail to do so, they can recover only that part of the loss that is not attributable to that failure. Of course, if the plaintiff can fully mitigate the loss, then the plaintiff has no claim to make other than the added expenses of mitigation.

In the United States, the *Hadley* rule was first cited with approval by an Iowa court. In the course of the next decade, it was adopted in other states, like Vermont, Massachusetts, Rhode Island, New York, Pennsylvania, and Wisconsin. Since 1900, it has been estimated that Baron Alderson's judgment has been referenced in more than four hundred American law review articles and in more than 270 judicial decisions. In 1981, the Texas Supreme Court affirmed that the decision remains the leading case on the assessment of contract damages. The wording of the Uniform Commercial Code, the governing source of most U.S. states' contract law, is drawn substantially from *Hadley*.

Of course, the more sophisticated contracting parties do not leave the calculation of damages to the courts but include in their contracts a set of detailed provisions to cover a range of eventualities. Nevertheless, as regards the *Hadley* rule itself, the courts have been busy trying to iron out any problems in its application to changing commercial conditions. It has been necessary for plaintiffs to establish that there is a genuine causal connection between their losses and the defendants' behavior; intervening actions or circumstances prevent recovery. However, it is the second limb of the test – that only extraordinary losses that arise in the parties' reasonable contemplation at the time of making the contract are recoverable – that has most occupied the courts' attention. Their efforts have been less than breathtaking.

In 1949, the courts had to determine whether a laundry firm that had ordered a new boiler, which arrived late, could recover for losses flowing from not being able to fulfill an exceptionally lucrative contact. It was held that, though the ordinary loss of profits was recoverable, those from the special contracts were not. Although the knowledge of the parties can be imputed and real (e.g., knowing the kind of business that the plaintiff was in is sufficient), it was imperative that both parties had the necessary knowledge of special circumstances when the contract was made. Again, in 1969, the court faced a situation in which a cargo of sugar was delivered late; in the meantime, the market price of sugar had fallen substantially. It was held that the lost profits could be recovered because the price volatility must have been in the reasonable contemplation of both parties when objectively assessed. In this case, Lord Reid emphasized that the standard of remoteness was to be interpreted as "not unlikely"; it allowed for considerably less than an even chance but more than it being very unusual. These subtleties are themselves often difficult to apply with any precision or predictability in the practical world.

One particularly perplexing challenge has been on the topic of unique performance. There are some contracts that are performed in a defective manner, but the cost of improvement or repair is disproportionate to the loss suffered. For instance, in a 1995 English case, a builder agreed to construct a swimming pool with a diving area of seven feet, six inches, deep. When constructed, the pool had a depth of only six feet. The cost of rebuilding the pool to the agreed depth would have been £21,560, which was almost as much as the original project. In contrast, the builder contended that the pool owner had suffered no loss and that the damages should be zero. The trial judge found that the resale value of the property had hardly diminished at all by reason of the shallower pool and that the pool owner had no intention of using the damages to reconstruct the pool anyway. An award of £2,500 was made for "a loss of amenity brought about by the shortfall in depth." The Court of Appeal set aside the decision and instead gave judgment for the entire cost of rebuilding. On further appeal to the House of Lords, it was held that, though the general rule should be the full cost of performance in accordance with the contractual specifications, only nominal damages were appropriate when the costs of repair were disproportionate to the benefit to be gained. In this case, the pool owner received the small difference between the enhanced value that the property would have had with a deeper pool and that with a shallower pool.

It should be clear, therefore, that, although the *Hadley* rule is an established star in the legal firmament, its precise import and application is far from fixed. And this is the beauty of Baron Alderson's ruling. Like Keats's "Endymion" or Pachelbel's *Canon*, it lends itself to a richness of interpretation; its greatness is not found in its fixity but in its fecundity. As the commercial and social context has changed over the past 150 years, the rule allows the judges to change with it. So the legal world of contract damages is illuminated by *Hadley*, but it is not a prisoner to it. This is a sign of its strength as a great case, not its weakness.

Pickford and Co. continues to thrive as a moving and storage service. The limiting of damages in the contract certainly did no harm to its economic growth. Joseph Baxendale ran the company until his death in 1872 as a very wealthy eighty-six-year-old: the company was left to his sons. It remains a household name in England, and its blue removal vans are still seen trundling along city streets and motorways. It was finally incorporated in 1901 and operates today as a publicly quoted company as part of the TEAM Group: it still has a branch office on Great Western Road in Gloucester. In a nice historical footnote, it should be noted that its Managing Director Kevin Pickford is a direct descendant of the Pickford family of the 1750s.

Joseph and Jonah Hadley sold City Mills a couple of years after the law case in 1860 and moved to London. They continued in the milling trade, and Jonah became recognized as a very accomplished innovator in developing apparatus for the improved and efficient cleaning of flour. City Mills was bought by Joseph Reynolds and Henry Allen and transferred to their sons in 1875. But the milling business had run into financial troubles; increased competition had reduced the price of flour. In 1886, it was sold to Charles Priday, who operated other mills in the area. However, as Gloucester port became too small to accommodate oceangoing ships, the flour trade declined. The mill was taken over by Spillers Milling, a subsidiary of the huge company Dalgety. It was eventually closed in March 1994. The buildings have since been converted into apartments.

However, on July 21, 2007, the Gloucester city authorities installed a plaque on what used to be City Flour Mills to commemorate the contracts case of *Hadley v. Baxendale*. It was unveiled by the mayor of Gloucester, Harjit Gill, and Francis Snyder, a Texas law professor and unofficial keeper of the *Hadley* flame. Reporting on this ceremony, the local

Figure 8.3. Joseph and Jonah Hadley's City Flour Mills, June 2005.

journalist Hugh Worsnip wrote that "this ruling has provided employment for lawyers and arguments in law schools throughout the world ever since." Over the years, it has produced more than just flour; it has produced much food for thought for lawyers and law students throughout the common world.

9

Of Crimes and Cautions

The Rights and Rites of Investigation

Andy Warhol's statement that "everyone gets their fifteen minutes of fame" is one of contemporary society's defining clichés. Although Warhol himself has far exceeded his allotted time slot, his dismissive remark captures our fascination with the fleeting, here-today-gone-tomorrow status of celebrity. It is as much a comment on people's limited attention span as it is on the nature of fame itself. However, there are some characters who transcend the fashions and fads of the moment and earn lasting renown. Although some earn fame through their worthy achievements, others carve out infamy for themselves by the turpitude of their deeds.

The criminal justice process has generated more than its fair share of infamous characters. Few do not know of Jack the Ripper or Al Capone; they have become the popular stuff of villainous imagery. Yet there are some who find their way into the public consciousness through less spectacular routes; they are memorialized in the details of law's sprawling narrative. One of those is Ernesto Miranda. He was a sad-sack, if schizophrenic, criminal who through force of circumstance and legal serendipity has left a lasting impression on police manuals and investigative behaviors. In a dubious legacy, the name *Miranda* has come to be intimately associated with the constitutional rights of criminal suspects.

Lois Ann Jameson was an eighteen-year-old woman in the warm 1963 spring of Phoenix, Arizona. Although she came across as shy and retiring, this was as much to do with her low IQ as with her temperament. She worked at her local Paramount Theater at one of its concession stands. On this March evening, the Second World War movie *The Longest Day* was playing. As befits its title, it had a running time of almost three hours. This meant that it was later than usual and close to midnight when Lois Ann got to leave the theater. After a short bus ride, she began the few minutes' walk to her home. She noticed a car following her. A man got out and approached her. Without further warning, the man grabbed her, put his hand over her mouth, and pulled her in to the backseat of the car. Once there, he tied her hands and ankles and put a knife to her throat.

That man was alleged to be Ernesto Arturo Miranda. Miranda, coming up to his twenty-third birthday a few

days later, had been on a sadly predictable arc. A child of
Mexican immigrants, he had lost his mother at an early
age. When his father remarried, he had never settled with
his new family. Beginning in the eighth grade, he had a
long record of petty offenses for which he had spent several periods in detention. Drifting from state to state in the
American Southwest, he tried to turn things around by join-
ing the army. But he received a dishonorable discharge after
serving six of fifteen months "at hard labor in the stock-
ade" for being absent without leave and for committing a
Peeping Tom offence. He moved in with a separated older
woman, Twila Hoffman, who already had two children; they
soon had a young daughter of their own. Heavily tattooed
and with a temporary laboring job at a local produce depot,
he was something of the stereotypical loser; he engendered
loathing and sympathy in equal parts.

Ernesto apparently drove Lois Ann out into the desert.
She was understandably confused about exactly what happened. Nevertheless, although muddled about the details
of her ordeal, she was clear that she had been raped at
knifepoint. He drove her back near her house on Citrus
Way, and when dropping her off, he made a pathetic plea
to "please pray for me." Disheveled and distressed on her
arrival at home, she told her family what had happened: the
police were called. That intercourse had occurred was confirmed at a later medical examination that night at the Good
Samaritan Hospital, even though there was little evidence
of any struggle or that she was sexually inexperienced, as

she claimed. With few leads to go on, the police made little progress in tracking down her assailant.

Lois Ann returned to work at the movie theater. Her brother-in-law, who lived with Lois Ann, her sister, and her mother met her at the bus stop and walked her home. A week later, they saw an old 1953 Packard car cruising near the bus stop and she told her brother-in-law that it looked like the one in which she had been abducted. He took down the licence-plate number of DFL 312. A police check revealed that there was no 1953 Packard licensed in this number, but that there was a car with the number DFL 317. It was registered in the name of Twila Hoffman, Miranda's live-in partner. With little delay, the police moved in, arrested Ernesto, and took him down to the police station.

The officers assigned to the case were Carroll Cooley and Wilfred Young. They were relatively seasoned detectives on the Phoenix force and had been assigned to investigate the alarming number of rapes that had been occurring in Lois Ann's neighborhood. The detectives arranged a hasty and ill-conceived lineup. Lois Ann was confronted by four men, all Mexican, all males, all the same age, and all the same height and build. Not surprisingly, she was unable to make a positive identification of any particular man and could confirm only that he looked like them all.

What followed was of crucial significance to the case and to later constitutional doctrine. Miranda was taken to a small interrogation room and questioned by Cooley and Young for a good two hours. Whether they simply hectored

Figure 9.1. Ernesto Miranda joins a lineup in March 1963 on the day of his infamous confession (Arizona State Library).

him into a confession for Lois Ann's rape and other offenses or whether they went further and made various threats to his safety and well-being is unclear. But the upshot was that he confessed to the rape of Lois Ann, as well as other rapes and robberies. She was hurriedly brought into the interrogation room and, when Miranda was asked if she was the woman he had assaulted, he said, "That's the girl."

At no point in his time at the police station was Miranda ever told about his constitutional rights. Under the U.S. Constitution's Fifth Amendment, he was not supposed to "be compelled in any criminal case to be a witness against himself," and under the Sixth Amendment, he was entitled "to have the assistance of counsel for his defence." Although there was considerable debate about exactly what protection these rights accorded to arrested persons and when they became available to them in the investigation process, it was accepted that Miranda had not been told by Officers Cooley and Young about them. It was later alleged that such a reminder was unnecessary in this case, as Miranda would clearly be aware of these rights from his frequent involvement in the criminal system.

After the interrogation and his identification of Lois Ann, Miranda was asked to write out and sign a formal confession. His statement verified many of the details that his victim had initially told the police – picked her up on the street near the bus stop, drove a few miles to the desert, tried to undress her, penetrated her slightly, drove her home, and asked her to say a prayer for him. At the top of the form on which he wrote his confession, there was a preprinted warning of rights, with a blank space for statement makers to include their names. It read:

> I, *Ernest A. Miranda*, do hereby swear that I make this statement voluntarily and of my own free will, with no threats, coercion, or promises of immunity, and with full knowledge of my legal rights, understanding any statement may be used against me.

As was customary, the indigent Miranda was assigned a state-paid lawyer. This was Alvin Moore. Admitted to the

Oklahoma bar in 1922 after a stint as a schoolteacher, he had come to Phoenix after serving as a lieutenant colonel in the infantry during the War. He had developed a relatively successful criminal defense practice. Over his career, Moore claimed to have defended more than thirty-five accused rapists and had compiled the astounding (and surely unbelievable) record of having failed to secure an acquittal for only one of them. However, he showed little genuine interest in Ernesto's case. This likely had something to do with the fact that, as well as taking an immediate dislike to Miranda, he was expected to do the trial and any subsequent appeal for the measly fee of $200. None of this augured well for Ernesto

In 1963, the law on police investigations and interrogations was in a state of flux. In the preceding decades, the courts had begun to take more seriously the rights of criminal suspects. Despite much criticism and opposition, the U.S. Supreme Court had led the way by challenging a variety of police methods and had begun to place some checks on their almost-unfettered power to do as they thought fit; just ends were considered to justify dubious means. In a series of cases beginning in the 1930s, as well as deciding that confessions were inadmissible at trial if "made in response to threats, promises, or inducements," the Court had begun to give sharper teeth to the Constitution's provisions about the need to provide counsel and the right against self-incrimination. In short, the law was beginning to establish a fairer balance between the broader need to preserve law and order and the desire to respect people's individual rights on arrest. Yet there was still much to be done and much to be clarified when Ernesto came to trial.

Miranda's trial took place at the Maricopa County Courthouse on June 20, 1963. Everyone involved saw it as an open-and-shut case that would take little time or effort. As well as calling a hesitant Lois Ann and the more experienced detectives as witnesses, Deputy Prosecutor Laurence Turoff entered his one and most compelling piece of evidence – Miranda's written confession. Moore made a halfhearted attempt to have the confession excluded on the basis that the accused had not been given an opportunity to consult a lawyer. But Judge Yale McFate was having none of it: the confession was duly entered in evidence, and the jury was directed to determine its voluntariness. In short order, the three women and nine men were unanimous in their verdict of guilty. Miranda was sentenced to twenty years' imprisonment.

Six months later, Miranda's appeal to the Arizona Supreme Court was heard. Moore sought a new trial on the basis that there was sufficient evidence on record to raise more than a reasonable doubt of Ernesto's guilt; the prosecution's main piece of evidence, Ernesto's confession, had been obtained improperly and ought to have been excluded from the jury's consideration. As well, he made the argument that was to gain much more traction with the

U.S. Supreme Court (and later constitutional law) than the Arizona courts – "Was Miranda afforded all the safeguards to his rights provided by the Constitution of the United States and the law and rules of the courts?"

The appeal court was unimpressed. On behalf of the court, Justice Ernest W. McFarland, a former Arizona governor and federal senator, took the strong line that, as Miranda had not requested counsel before or during his interrogation by the police officers, he was in no position to raise this failing later to query the validity and admissibility of his confession. Moreover, Justice McFarlane held that the recent and confusing *Escobedo* ruling (in which the Supreme Court had held that criminal suspects might be able to claim a right to counsel during some interrogations) did not apply; therefore, Miranda's confession was properly and fairly admitted into evidence. With that, he upheld the jury's verdict and refused the request for a new trial. Miranda was realistically facing a very long stay in Arizona's penitentiaries.

As is so often the case, fate intervened to play a strong hand in Ernesto's life. In the same way that May Donoghue found her guardian angel in Walter Leechman (see Chapter 6), so Ernesto was unexpectedly (and perhaps undeservingly) blessed with the appearance of his own champion. Robert J. Corcoran ran the Phoenix office of the American Civil Liberties Union (ACLU). A former district attorney and later Arizona judge himself, he was very familiar with the Arizona law and police practice around interrogations.

While trawling through the notices in the Pacific Reporter, a lawyers' reference periodical, he came across the *Miranda* case. In a fortuitous and astute piece of initiative, he thought that it would be an ideal case through which to advance the progressive agenda of the ACLU on expanding criminals' rights by appealing it to the U.S. Supreme Court.

Corcoran first sought to enlist Alvin Moore in his crusade, but Moore had lost even the small appetite that he had for further involvement. So Corcoran next turned to Rex E. Lee. He was an up-and-coming young Phoenix lawyer who had been a law clerk to Justice Byron White of the Supreme Court when the *Escobedo* case had been decided. Although Lee was very keen to get involved and immediately recognized the huge potential of *Miranda*'s facts and findings for developing the law, he had to decline because of a Supreme Court rule that prohibited ex-clerks from appearing before it as counsel for at least two years.

Undeterred, Corcoran's next port of call was the offices of John J. Flynn. A military veteran and committed social activist, he was the chief trial attorney at Lewis, Roca, Scoville, Beauchamps, and Linton, one of Phoenix's largest and most reputable law firms. He had a reputation for being an articulate advocate who assumed a powerful persona both in and out of court. Under a standing arrangement with the ACLU whereby the firm agreed to take a couple of *pro bono* cases per year, Flynn accepted the assignment with relish. He brought his older colleague John P. Frank on board. More scholarly and reflective than Flynn, Frank had been a law clerk to Justice Hugo Black of the Supreme Court in the early 1940s. He had left a lucrative East Coast career and moved to Arizona to help his chronic asthma. With Frank doing the writing and Flynn doing the speaking, they made a wonderful team and set about redressing the plight of vulnerable prisoners in police custody.

When Ernesto received a letter from Corcoran telling him of this good news, he wrote back to him from his prison cell with gratitude and a renewed hope: "Your letter has made me very happy.... To know that someone has taken an interest in my case, has increased my moral [*sic*] enormously.... I would appreciate if you or either Mr. Flynn keep me informed of any and all results. I also want to thank you and Mr. Flynn for all that you are doing for me." Perhaps he was beginning to receive those strokes of good fortune that had so far eluded him through his life.

The *Miranda v. Arizona* appeal was heard by the U.S. Supreme Court over three days at the end of February 1966. In a standard practice, the appeal had been consolidated with three other appeals (*Westover v. United States*, *Vignera v. State of New York*, and *State of California v. Stewart*) on similar facts and rulings. There were fifty-eight lawyers from fourteen states who participated in submitting written briefs to the Court or who made oral arguments to the justices. The central legal issue was whether law enforcement officials had to advise suspects in custody of their right to remain silent and to obtain an attorney. If they did, this would demand a fundamental change in police methods and ultimately in the trials of criminals like Ernesto.

Oral argument before the Supreme Court tends to be a spirited affair and, unlike in other more formal jurisdictions, the exchanges between judges and counsel can become quite heated. The hearing in *Miranda* was an absorbing drama for the uncommitted observer. John Flynn went first. Adding powerful rhetoric to Frank's finely crafted written brief, he made a rousing defense of the Constitution's protections and urged the Court to take them more seriously than it had previously done; they must be given as much practical effect as abstract acknowledgment. In a lively exchange with Justice Potter Stewart, he emphasized that, if there was a right to counsel, then suspects deserve to be told about this at the earliest opportunity; it was not a right that should be reserved for the rich or the educated. It was an uncompromising and bold presentation.

In response, Arizona's assistant attorney general Gary Nelson gave no quarter. In a forceful reliance on legal principle, he pointed out that any further checks on the activities of enforcement officials were unwarranted and would adversely affect the efficacy of the criminal justice system in apprehending and convicting serious rapists and murderers. He hinted at the Court having the decisive role of reconciling the powers of good and evil. In particular, he made a strong case for distinguishing Ernesto's situation from others. Whereas the defendant in *Escobedo* was a neophyte in the criminal courts and had been deceived by the police, Ernesto was a hardened criminal who knew what was what. A cameo role was played by Thurgood Marshall (see Chapter 5) who was now President Johnson's appointment as the first African American U.S. solicitor general. Somewhat against character, he was obliged to defend the administration's need to restrict the circumstances in which the government was to pay for counsel for indigent suspects.

The Supreme Court took time to consider its judgment. As remains the custom, the judges delivered their decision before the end of the Court's term. So, on Monday, June 13, 1966, Chief Justice Earl Warren (see Chapter 5) read aloud the full, sixty-page opinion. It was a 5–4 decision in favor of Miranda; a new trial was ordered. The chief justice was joined by Justices Hugo Black, William Douglas, Abe Fortas, and William Brennan. There were three dissenting judgments; Justice John Harlan's opinion was joined by Justice Potter Stewart. Justice Byron White and Tom Clark gave separate dissenting opinions. It was hardly a recipe for clarity and confidence.

In his lead judgment, the chief justice put his considerable weight and influence behind the push for extended rights for criminal suspects. This was quite a turnaround for a person who had spent part of his early legal career as a state prosecutor in Alameda County, California. However, putting that experience to good use, he drew heavily from police manuals, many of which had not been referenced by the parties' lawyers. Refusing to go as far as the ACLU's proposal that there should be a station lawyer present at all interrogations, he laid out a set of new guidelines for all interrogations that, if broken, would lead to the inadmissibility of any tainted confession:

> The person in custody must, prior to interrogation, be clearly informed that he has the right to remain silent, and that anything he says will be used against him in court; he must be clearly informed that he has the right to consult with a lawyer and to have the lawyer with him during interrogation, and that, if he is indigent, a lawyer will be appointed to represent him.

In his dissent, Justice Clark was not entirely opposed to the extension of constitutional rights to criminal suspects. More conservative than the majority, he cautioned restraint, "lest we go too far too fast." Instead, he wanted to steer clear of absolute rules and preferred a more holistic approach that was modeled on the judgment the year earlier of Justice Arthur Goldberg in the *Haynes* case. Justice Clark thought that, if a police officer failed to offer appropriate warnings about the suspect's right to have a lawyer present in any interrogation, "the burden would be on the State to prove that counsel was knowingly and intelligently waived or that, in the totality of the circumstances, including the failure to give the necessary warnings, the confession was clearly voluntary." In this tread-lightly view, Ernesto's confession would not be automatically excluded but might be if the prosecution could not meet its burden.

Justice Harlan felt no compunction to hold his fire. He invoked the telling words of Justice Robert H. Jackson from an earlier generation, to the effect that "this Court is forever adding new stories to the temples of constitutional law, and the temples have a way of collapsing when one story too many is added." Hitting his stride, he took direct aim at his activist colleagues and contended that they had gone much too far in their ACLU-inspired drive to invigorate the rights of criminals against the police and the public interest. He was insistent:

> Nothing in the letter or the spirit of the Constitution or in the precedents squares with the heavy-handed and one-sided action that is so precipitously taken by the Court in the name of fulfilling its constitutional responsibilities.

The overall effect of the *Miranda* decision and its warring judgments most certainly set the liberal cat among the conservative pigeons. The law-and-order lobby was up in arms and future president Richard Nixon railed against the decision and its implications; it was seen as indiscriminately besmirching the good name of all police officers and giving dangerous criminals and their attorneys far too strong a hand. Others welcomed the decision and saw it as further confirmation of the country's commitment to uphold the liberal promise of its constitutional guarantees. Either way, Ernesto Miranda's name soon passed into common usage: it became commonplace for police and others to talk about the need to "mirandize" suspects.

Miranda was not only an ending to one era of constitutional law but also a beginning to another new era. As resounding and as assertive as the Supreme Court's decision had been, it left as many questions as answers. As do all great cases, it settled one set of issues only to reopen another equally problematic set of topics. Over the intervening decades, the courts have sought to bring some clarity to the use and effect of Miranda warnings. Although the Supreme Court retains ultimate authority as the arbiter of the Constitution's demands, criminal investigation is a largely state-regulated matter, and there have developed some significant variations across the United States. Even at the Supreme Court level, as its judicial personnel has changed and the tenor of the times has shifted, there still remains considerable debate about the reach and rigor of criminal suspects' rights under interrogation.

Opposition to *Miranda* gained sufficient force and momentum such that, in 1968, Congress sought to limit its impact. As part of an omnibus package of measures in the Crime Control and Safe Street Act, Congress attempted to abandon the strict protocol of Chief Justice Warren's judgment and revert to an approach that looked to "the totality of circumstances" more along the lines envisaged by Justice

Clark. Because this provision was an act of the federal Congress, it applied only to federal criminal proceedings and those that occurred in the District of Columbia. With some reluctance, a less liberal bench of the Supreme Court determined in 2000 in *Dickerson* that its *Miranda* ruling remained good law and that the offending section of the federal statute must be struck down. An armed bank robber was successful in having his statements to an FBI officer rendered inadmissible, as he had not received his Miranda warnings.

Today, it should come as little surprise to learn, therefore, that the law is still fluid. Although the courts have worked within Chief Justice Warren's principled framework, Harlan's totality-of-circumstances approach has succeeded in playing an important, if implicit, role. In developing this frontline area of legal regulation, where the doctrinal rubber hits the hard road of daily practice, the most pressing matters have been the following:

- *When do the rights kick in?* A person need only be warned of their rights when they are to be interrogated; the location of the interrogation is not determinative, but the fact that an interrogation is taking place is. This means that statements made while an arrest is in progress and before the Miranda warning was given or completed are generally admissible. However, the need to give Miranda warnings does not preclude the police from asking standard booking questions about the suspect's name, date of birth, address, and the like. Also, Miranda warnings do not need to be given when an imminent threat to public safety exists.

- *Who is required to issue warnings?* It has to be demonstrated that the person conducting the interrogation was a known state agent. This obviously includes all police officers and law enforcement officials but does not extend to private citizens. The use of an undercover police officer or a paid informant as an intermediary does not violate the *Miranda* rule. Although private security guards are not state agents, they may become so treated if an off-duty police officer is moonlighting as one.

- *Does any particular phrasing or order of words need to be used?* Although most police and enforcement officers have tended to use very specific and approved language, the courts have not insisted on Miranda rights being read in any particular order or that they must be couched in any particular verbal formula. Focus has come to be placed on a practical and broad inquiry into whether the availability of those rights have been adequately and fully conveyed to the detained person.

- *What counts as a valid waiver?* Any subsequent waiver of Miranda rights by a criminal suspect must be "knowing, intelligent, and voluntary." However, this has been restricted to little more than ensuring that the suspect appears to have a reasonable grasp that what he or she is doing is waiving known rights and that he or she is not being coerced into signing the waiver.

- *What about other evidence that results from an invalid interrogation?* This is known as the doctrine of the fruits of the poisonous tree. Although a confession might be inadmissible, the police may have been able to discover other nontestimonial evidence (e.g., a weapon, a piece of property) as a result of the defendant's admissions. Although there are some minor exceptions, the admissibility of any derivative evidence is not affected: the prosecution still have to prove that the evidence is connected to the defendant without reference to the excluded confession. Also, the prosecution may still use a *Miranda*-excluded confession as a prior inconsistent statement to impeach the credibility of a defendant's testimony if the defendant takes the stand at trial and offers a different account of events.

As will be clear, the precise meaning and implementation of the *Miranda* decision has become a battleground where liberals and conservatives join issue. Although this particular engagement has a distinctly American flavor to it, other developed countries have also grappled with the tension between law and order and criminal suspect's rights. Although there are important differences in the details, there is a surprising level of general agreement about the need to protect suspects from abusive interrogations by officials through obligatory warnings and exclusionary rules of evidence. Of course, the proof of the pudding is in the eating – to what extent are courts and justice systems prepared to enforce these standards when, as with Ernesto, the defendant is much more likely guilty than not?

The Supreme Court's decision gave some hope to Ernesto, deserved or otherwise. He was granted his retrial in February 1967 for the rape of Lois Ann Jameson. The defense was conducted by John Flynn himself before out-of-county judge Laurence T. Wren who had been brought in to ensure some local balance and independence. The five-day trial was largely taken up with legal argument about the status and admissibility of different pieces of evidence and testimony. When the legal dust settled, the *Miranda* guidelines were strictly followed. Led by Bob Corbin, Arizona's attorney general, the prosecution was permitted to call Lois Ann as a witness; she gave a rather muddled account of what happened. But no mention of the confession or of her identification of Ernesto at the police station was allowed. With such a bare-bones case against him, it looked like Ernesto would be acquitted.

But the past and Ernesto's poor judgment managed to catch up with him; his own refusal to remain silent worked against him. Anticipating an acquittal in the retrial, he had complained to the welfare authorities about his common law wife's lack of care for their daughter shortly before the retrial was scheduled to begin. Twila Hoffman was far from happy. And like a woman scorned, she unleashed her fury against

Ernesto. She located and told the still-involved Detective Cooley that she had visited Miranda in jail on March 16, 1963, three days after his arrest on the original rape charge. Twila claimed that, in a conversation with her, Ernesto had admitted to raping Lois Ann Jameson. This was the most damning of evidence. Most important, there would be no barrier to this new confession's admission in evidence as Twila was not a law enforcement officer and had no connection to the authorities at all. For the prosecution, this was a godsend.

With suitable drama, Corbin surprised Flynn with the announcement of Hoffman's proposed testimony about another confession by Ernesto. Although Flynn argued fervently that the common law marriage precluded Hoffman's testimony or at least reduced its credibility, Judge Wren disagreed and allowed Hoffman to testify. Flynn knew that this would have a massive and negative impact on the jury and would do much to corroborate Lois Ann's shaky testimony. And so it did. Despite Flynn's efforts to discredit her testimony on cross-examination, the jury reached a guilty verdict in slightly more than an hour and Miranda was sentenced again to twenty years' imprisonment. A second appeal to the state's supreme court was dismissed and Ernesto returned to prison with no future hope of acquittal. It was exactly one year from his successful appeal to the U.S. Supreme Court. For some, this was a poetic and fitting end to Ernesto's case – the police had been obliged to alter their interrogation techniques by respecting suspects' constitutional rights, but the unlikable Ernesto himself had been convicted, and Lois Ann's personal reputation, if not her physical integrity, had been substantially restored.

Ernesto remained in the Arizona State Penitentiary until he received early parole in December 1972 after several rejected applications. In the years that followed, he continued his criminal ways; he was arrested several times for a variety of minor offenses. In a piece of questionable entrepreneurship, he started autographing Miranda warning cards at fairs and other venues for a couple of dollars. He spent time back in prison for violating his parole after being arrested on gun possession charges. After his release, Ernesto reverted to his drifter ways and hung out in bars and hotels in the seedier neighborhoods of Phoenix. However, in January 1967, Ernesto's already low stock of luck ran out. He was involved in a card game at the shady La Amapola Bar. A fight broke out over a disputed debt of $3 and Ernesto was stabbed in the stomach and chest. At thirty-four years old, he was pronounced dead on arrival at the same Good Samaritan Hospital where Lois Ann had been taken years before after the rape.

But there was still another ironic sting in Ernesto's tale. A short time after the stabbing, the police detained Fernando Rodriquez and Eseziquel Moreno on suspicion of Ernesto's stabbing. However, they refused to cooperate and the police officers had a hard time getting them to say much at all. With little hard evidence to go on, Rodriquez and Moreno were soon released: they both disappeared (perhaps

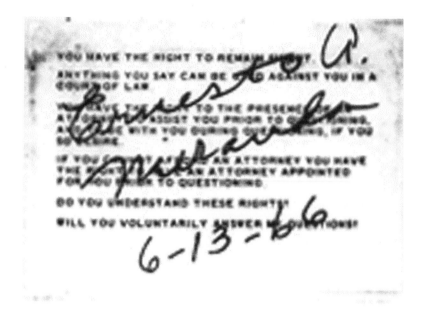

Figure 9.2. After Miranda was released from jail he autographed Miranda cards for $1.50 a piece.

to Mexico) and were never seen around Phoenix again. And the reason they kept quiet? When they were detained, the police acted exactly as the chief justice of the United States would have wanted them to – they were read the Miranda warning in Spanish and advised of their right to remain silent. No one was ever charged with the hapless Ernesto's death.

10

Coming up for Air

The Common Law at 2010

Whatever else it might be or have, the common law has legs. It remains a vibrant force that has managed to retain its prominence and rigor through dint of its stamina and versatility. It is obviously not a "thing of beauty" that is "a joy for ever" whose "loveliness increases" – it very much has its sore spots, unsightly features, and ugly postures. But a little like Keats' conception of beauty, the common law likely "will never pass into nothingness." It has exhibited a tenacity and a familiarity that has enabled it to maintain the allegiance of its professional corps, who in turn have succeeded sufficiently to convince people, high and low, that it is an institutional practice worth preserving. The common law is a showcase or a shambles, depending on your point of view, by virtue of the talents of those lawyers who work with it and the interests of those litigants who must rely on it.

There are some true believers who insist that the common law, a little like the market, is much more than the sum of its discrete decisions. Following the lead of a Lord Mansfield (who, at the time, was still Mr. Murray, a young solicitor general) in an eighteenth-century case, such true believers opine that "the common law works itself pure by rules drawn from the fountain of justice." In this lofty account, the common law is cast as both the expression and repository of a political insight that transcends the bounds of its temporary articulation – there is a balance between the law's immanence (i.e., the idea of law as the rational embodiment of an indwelling justice) and the law's instrumentality (i.e., the practice of using law as an institutional tool for settling social problems).

This is a very grand vision that is surely belied by the biographies and circumstances of great cases. The American judge and renaissance figure Oliver Wendell Holmes, Jr. seems nearer the mark in his assessment that "the life of the law has not been logic, but experience." It is an experience that captures a more workaday approach than an abstract refinement. As the trajectory and fate of great cases attest, no legal doctrine is borne of logic alone. The best that can be hoped for is that doctrines might develop that are successful in the sense that they serve particular purposes, that they adapt to local conditions, and that they have a certain flexibility to remain relevant in a changed environment. However, whether particular rules are good or bad or useful or useless is a local assessment; it is not a once-and-for-all judgment about the rules' universal desirability – and certainly not an evaluation of its logical or pure form. Although common law decisions are the product of individual judges' best efforts to be rational and just, this does not mean that there is some invisible hand at work that coordinates and integrates the mass of cases into a unifying whole.

Contrary to the wishes of its true believers, progress or success is not about the common law becoming more objective and logical or about achieving a purer form of justice that somehow transcends the disabling influences of interests, commitments, fuzziness, history, culture, and ideology. As great cases show, there is no real basis for dallying with Mansfield's juristic ghost and his still many contemporary disciples about the common law working itself pure; it is much more instructive and much more authentic to think about judges as engaged, through their own efforts and imagination, in the process of law simply working itself against and within local conditions. Sometimes, they do well, and other times, they do not. After all, judges are merely ordinary persons doing a difficult job under difficult circumstances; they are not the demigods or philosopher-monarchs that many would have them be. The common law is no better or worse than the lawyers, judges, and commentators who comprise its dramatis personae.

By approaching the common law primarily as a living social and historical artifact (with all the foibles and flaws that this entails), there are a whole host of fresh insights that will be opened up and a slew of old prejudices that will be confirmed. Looking back at those great cases that I have introduced and explored in this book, some of the more prominent and obvious ones that come to mind are the following:

- *Fixing the Facts* – Much of the crucial adjudicative work is done in determining exactly what happened. How the facts are presented by the lawyers and how the judges decide what version to believe are often decisive in the final outcome. Although much is based on the availability and credibility of evidence, the main factual findings are often made with a strong eye on what the law considers important and relevant; the factual cloth is often cut to suit the legal purpose.

- *On- and Offstage* – As with most dramatic productions, it is often as important to know what went on offstage as what actually gets onstage. Although the judgments represent the public face of the law, there is so much else that needs to be appreciated to understand the institutional context, the practical compromises, the failed rehearsals, and the competing personalities that went into the final staging. String pulling is not an unknown aspect of the common law.

- *Show Me the Money* – As everyone knows, litigation is an expensive business. It is not only the most deserving litigants and worthiest cases that find their way before the courts. The haves have a much better shot at justice than the have-nots, because they can hire the best lawyers and survive the long and attritional war of litigation. Unless ordinary people are lucky enough to find a legal champion or activist organization to help, their cause often will go unheeded by the courts.

- *Being Connected* – As with so much else, it is often who you know as much as what you know that will count the most. Perhaps more than most communities, law is made up of various webs of interconnecting interests and relationships; these connections overlap with other professional, commercial, and particularly political networks. There is considerable traffic between the judicial, legislative, and executive arm of government so that a shared outlook and attitude toward problems and issues often develops.

- *Never Say Die* – The common law offers an object lesson in how persistence is a vital attribute of the successful litigant. "If at first you don't succeed, then appeal" seems to be a necessary mantra for those who intend to change the law or vindicate their cause. Mindful that this will increase considerably the expense of litigation, it is only the well-funded few who can manage to survive the long slog of hearings that will be required.

- *All in the Timing* – As is comedy, the common law is all about timing. In so many situations, much depends on the right people being in the right place at the right time. Even good cases with good lawyers will not succeed unless they manage to get the right judges and all the political stars are in alignment. The common law tends to follow, not lead, extant social forces and values.

• *Taking a Chance* – Although the courts are one of society's favored venues for reasoned argument and informed debate about important social and moral issues, there is so much that simply comes down to serendipity. In almost all great cases, one side or the other benefited from a stroke of good fortune. Of course, although it requires talent and dedication to take advantage of it, there is always an element of luck in play.

When the common law is approached through the lens of great cases, it is hard to resist the conclusion that the common law tradition is more an open and creative one in which anything might go than a bounded and cautious one. One of the few constants in law and adjudication is that change and stability are maintained through continuous acts of revision: transformation is the lifeblood of the common law's vibrant tradition. Great cases show how the law develops by breaking with its past; they confound the idea that the common law develops incrementally and logically. To be in praise of great cases is a tribute to the force of Holmes's observation that "continuity with the past is only a necessity, not a duty." And, judging from the history of its development through great cases, the common law has and continues to impose a duty on its personnel to respect the past best by revolutionizing it in regular acts of continuing transformation.

In drawing up such an inventory of the common law's practical qualities and distinguishing features, it should be apparent that I do not intend to contribute to the cult of the common law. The glorification of the common law as an exemplary process for resolving difficult disputes and developing the law that is somehow superior to more comprehensive legislative and political interventions is to be strenuously resisted. There is nothing magical or miraculous about the common law as a decision-making process and body of substantive rules that it throws up. As my account about great cases hopefully reveals, the methods used and the results produced are variable in style and appeal; judicial decisions cover the whole range of political possibilities and work within a considerable set of institutional parameters. The common law is simply another governmental location at which officials struggle to forge workable solutions to demanding controversies. Whether societies should persist with such a process is a matter not of technical expertise but of political preference. If the common law is to continue in its privileged role, it will work best if it is stripped of its priestly trappings and viewed as the pragmatic, public, and corrigible practice that it is.

Bibliography

Chapter 1

Balkin, J. and Levinson, S. "The Canons of Constitutional Law." *Harvard Law Review* 111 (1997–1998): 963–1025.

Bobbitt, Philip C. *Constitutional Interpretation*. Oxford and Cambridge, MA: Blackwell Publishers, 1991.

Gilmore, Doug. *The Death of Contract*. Columbus, OH: The Ohio State University Press, 1974.

Holmes, Oliver Wendell, Jr. *The Common Law*. Boston: Little, Brown, and Company, 1881.

Hutchinson, Allan C. *Evolution and the Common Law*. New York: Cambridge University Press, 2005.

McLoughlin v. O'Brian, [1983] 1 AC 410 at 430 per Lord Scarman.

Warren, Samuel. *A Popular and Practical Introduction to Law Studies*. Philadelphia: John S. Littell, 1835.

Chapter 2

Biber, Katherine. "Cannibals and Colonialism." *Sydney Law Review* 27.4 (2005): 623–639.

Donahue, James. "Strange Prophetic Story By Edgar Allan Poe." The Mind of James Donohue. http://perdurabo10.tripod.com/warehousea/id42.html (accessed 7 June 2009).

Fairall, Paul Ames. "Reflections on Necessity as a Justification for Torture." *James Cook University Law Review* 11 (2004): 21–36.

Hanson, Neil. *The Custom of the Sea*. New York: John Wiley & Sons, Inc., 1999.

Harding, John. *Sailing's Strangest Moments: Extraordinary but True Stories from Over Three Centuries*. London: Chrysalis Books Group, 2004.

Martel, Yann. "How Richard Parker Came to Get His Name." Amazon. http://www.amazon.com/gp/feature.html?ie=UTF8&docId= 309590 (accessed 28 April 2009).

Moreton, Cole. "He wanted some adventure on the high seas. His shipmates ate him." *The Independent* 28 July 1996.

Norrie, Alan. *Crime, Reason and History: A Critical Introduction to Criminal Law (Law in Context)*. Cambridge: Cambridge University Press, 2001.

Quigley, Christine. *The Corpse: A History*. Jefferson, NC: McFarland & Company, Inc., 1996.

Robinson, Paul H. and Michael T. Cahill. *Law Without Justice: Why Criminal Law Doesn't Give People What They Deserve*. Oxford: Oxford University Press, 2005.

Simmons, James C. *Castaway in Paradise*. Dobbs Ferry, NY: Sheridan House, 1993.

Simpson, A. W. Brian. *Cannibalism and the Common Law: The Story of the Tragic Last Voyage of the Mignonette and the Strange Legal Proceedings to Which It Gave Rise*. Chicago: The University of Chicago Press, 1984.

Stilgoe, John R. *Lifeboat*. Charlottesville, VA: University of Virginia Press, 2007.

Whitman, James Q. *The Origins of Reasonable Doubt: Theological Roots of the Criminal Trial*. Orwigsburg, PA: Yale University Press, 2008.

Chapter 3

Black, Conrad. *Duplessis*. Toronto: McClelland and Stewart, 1977.

Dyzenhaus, David. "The Deep Structure of Roncarelli v. Duplessis." *University of New Brunswick Law Journal* 5 (2004): 111–124.

Kaplan, William. *Canadian Maverick: The Life and Times of Ivan C. Rand*. Toronto: The Osgoode Society for Canadian Legal History/The University of Toronto Press, 2009.

Sarra-Bournet, Michel. *L'affaire Roncarelli: Duplessis contra les Temoins de Jehovah.* Québec: Institut Québécois de recherche sur la culture, 1986.

Sheppard, Claude-Armand. "Roncarelli v. Duplessis: Art. 1053 C.C. Revolutionized." *McGill Law Journal* 6 (1960): 75–89.

Laporte, Pierre. *The True Face of Duplessis.* Montreal: Harvest House, 1960.

"Maurice Duplessis." CBC Digital Archives. Radio Canada. http://archives.cbc.ca/politics/provincial_territorial_politics/topics/1461/ (accessed 23 May 2009).

Paulin, Marguerite. *Maurice Duplessis: Powerbroker, Politician.* Montreal: XYZ Publishing, 2005.

Chapter 4

Baker, Sandra E. and David W. MacDonald. "Foxes and Foxhunting on Farms in Wiltshire: A Case Study." *Journal of Rural Studies* 16.2 (2000): 185–201.

Bennett, Julie. "Is There Room for You in a Rich Playground?" *The Wall Street Journal*, 16 March 2004. http://www.realestatejournal.com/buysell/regionalnews/20040316-bennett.html (accessed 16 July 2009).

Benson, Marjorie L. and Marie-Ann Bowden. *Understanding Property: A Guide to Canada's Property Law.* Scarborough: Carswell Thomson Professional Publishing, 1997.

Berger, Bethany. "It's Not About the Fox: The Untold History of Pierson v. Post." *Duke Law Journal* 55 (2006): 1089–1144.

Bollier, David. *Silent Theft: The Private Plunder of Our Common Wealth.* New York: Routledge, 2003.

Burke, Barlow and Joseph Snoe. *Property: Examples & Explanations*, 3rd edition. New York: Wolters Kluwer Law & Business, 2008.

Dharmapala, Dhammika and Rohan Pitchford. "An Economic Analysis of 'Riding to Hounds': Pierson v. Post Revisited." *The Journal of Law, Economics, and Organization* 18.1 (2002): 39–66.

Fernandez, Angela. "The Lost Record of Pierson v. Post, the Famous Fox Case." *Law and History Review* 27.1 (2009): 149–178.

———. "The Pushy Pedagogy of Pierson v. Post and the Fading Federalism of James Kent." http://www.law.utoronto.ca/documents/fernandez/PiersonPostAbstract.pdf (accessed 14 July 2009).

Freyfogle, Eric T. and Dale D. Goble. *Wildlife Law: A Primer.* Washington, D.C.: Island Press, 2009.

Gordon, Thomas F. and Douglas Walton. "Pierson vs. Post Revisited: A Reconstruction Using the Carneades Argumentation Framework." *Proceeding of the 2006 Conference on Computational Models of Argument* (2006): 208–219.

Gray, Brian E. "Report and Recommendations on the Law of Capture and First Possession." http://web.mac.com/graybe/Site/Writingsfiles/Hayashi%20Brief.pdf (accessed 14 July 2009).

Marvin, Garry. "A Passionate Pursuit: Foxhunting as Performance." *Sociological Review* 51.s2 (2004): 46–60.

McDowell, Andrea. "Legal Fictions in Pierson v. Post." *Michigan Law Review* 105.4 (2006–2007): 735–779.

Murphy, Dean E. "A Ball in the Hand Is Worth a Lot – to the Lawyers." *The New York Times*, 16 October 2002. http://www.nytimes.com/2002/10/16/us/a-ball-in-the-hand-is-worth-a-lot-to-the-lawyers.html (accessed 14 July 2009).

Pierson, Richard E. and Jennifer Pierson. *Pierson Millennium*. Westminster, MD: Heritage Books, 1997.

Ziff, Bruce. *Principles of Property Law*, 4th edition. Toronto: Thomson Carswell, 2006.

Chapter 5

Anderson, Karen. *Little Rock: Race and Resistance at Central High School*. Princeton: Princeton University Press, 2009.

"Brown v. Board of Education." http://en.wikipedia.org/w/index.php?title=Brown_v._Board_of_Education&oldid=304710401 (accessed 28 July 2009).

Brown Foundation for Educational Equity, Excellence and Research. Brown v. Board of Education Myths v. Truths. http://Brownvboard.org/mythsandtruths/ (accessed 03 June 2009).

Cottrol, Robert J., Raymond T. Diamond, and Leland B. Ware. *Brown v. Board Of Education: Caste, Culture, and The Constitution*. Lawrence, KS: The University Press of Kansas, 2003.

Harbaugh, William Henry. *Lawyer's Lawyer: The Life of John W. Davis*. New York: Oxford University Press, 1990.

Kluger, Richard. *Simple Justice: The History of Brown v. Board of Education and Black America's Struggle for Equality*. New York: Alfred A. Knopf, 1976.

Patterson, James T. *Brown v. Board of Education: A Civil Rights Milestone and Its Troubled Legacy*. New York: Oxford University Press, 2002.

Smithsonian National Museum of American History, Behring Center. "Separate is Not Equal: Brown v. Board of Education." http://americanhistory.si.edu/brown/index.html (accessed 05 June 2009).

Telgen, Diane. *Brown v. Board of Education*. Detroit: Omnigraphics, Inc., 2005.

Wilkinson, J. Harvie III. *From Brown to Bakke: The Supreme Court and School Integration 1954–1978*. New York: Oxford University Press, 1979.

Wolters, Raymond. *The Burden of Brown: Thirty Years of School Desegregation*. Knoxville, TN: University of Tennessee Press, 1984.

Chapter 6

Burns, Peter T. and Susan J. Lyons. *Donoghue v. Stevenson and the Modern Law of Negligence: The Paisley Papers: The Proceedings of the Paisley Conference on the Law of Negligence*. Vancouver: The Continuing Legal Education Society of British Columbia, 1991.

Council of Paisley. Paisley. http://paisley.org.uk (accessed 15 June 2009).

Heuston, R. F. V. *Lives of the Lord Chancellors 1885–1940*. London: Oxford University Press, 1964.

Lewis, Geoffrey. *Lord Atkin*. Portland: Hart Publishing, 1999.

Oxford Dictionary of National Biography. Oxford: Oxford University Press, 2004.

Samuels, Alec. "James Richard Atkin, Lord Atkin of Aberdovey Tribute." *Cambrian Law Review* 25 (1994): 147–151.

Taylor, M. R. "The Good Neighbour on Trial: A Message from Scotland." *University of British Columbia Law Review* 17 (1983): 59–67.

The Paisley Snail. Dirs. David Hay, Martin Taylor and Chuck Garrows. 1996.

Chapter 7

Butt, Peter and Robert Eagleson. *Mabo, Wik, & Native Title*. Sydney: The Federation Press, 1998.

Loos, Noel. *Edward Koiki Mabo: His Life and Struggle for Land Rights*. St. Lucia: University of Queensland Press, 2004.

Mabo: Life of an Island Man. Dir. Trevor Graham. Lindfield, NSW: Film Australia. 1997.

"Mabo v. Queensland (No 1)." http://en.wikipedia.org/wiki/Mabo_v_Queensland_(No_1) (accessed 26 June 2009).

Bibliography

Mabo: The Native Title Revolution Website. Screen Australia Digital Learning. (n.d.). http://www.mabonativetitle.com/home.shtml (accessed 23 July 2009).

Russell, Peter H. *Recognizing Aboriginal Title: The Mabo Case and Indigenous Resistance to English-Settler Colonialism*. Toronto: University of Toronto Press, 2005.

Sharp, Nonie. *No ordinary judgment: Mabo, the Murray Islander's land case*. Canberra: Aboriginal Studies Press, 1996.

Chapter 8

Anderson, Roy Ryden. "Of Mack Trucks, Road Bugs, Gilmore and Danzig: Happy Birthday Hadley v. Baxendale Symposium: The Common Law of Contracts as a World Force in Two Ages of Revolution: Foreseeability and Damages." *Texas Wesleyan Law Review* 11 (2004–2005): 431–455.

Blumberg, Phillip I. "Limited Liability and Corporate Groups." *Journal of Corporation Law* 11 (1985–1986): 573–633.

Bryer, R. A. "The Mercantile Laws Commission of 1854 and the Political Economy of Limited Liability." *Economic History Review* 50.1 (1997): 37–56.

Conway-Jones, A. H. "The Warehouse of Gloucester Docks." *Gloucestershire Society for Industrial Archaeology Journal* (1977–1978): 13–19.

Conway-Jones, Hugh. "Gloucester Docks." April 2003. http://www.gloucesterdocks.me.uk/studies/pridaysmill.htm (accessed 17 July 2009).

Cushman, Robert Frank and James J. Myers. *Construction Law Handbook*. New York: Aspen Law & Business, 2001.

Danzig, Richard. "Hadley v. Baxendale: A Study in the Industrialization of the Law." *Journal of Legal Studies* 4 (1975): 249–284.

European Route of Industrial Heritage. National Waterways Museum and Gloucester Dock. http://www.erih.net/anchor-points/detail.html?user_erihobjects_pi2[showUid]=15249&cHash=aec0985a1e (accessed 29 June 2009).

Faust, Florian. "Hadley v. Baxendale – An Understandable Miscarriage of Justice." *Journal of Legal History* 15.1 (1994): 41–72.

Fishman, James J. "Joseph Baxendale Symposium: The Common Law of Contracts as a World Force in Two Ages of Revolution: A Conference Celebrating the 150th Anniversary of Hadley v. Baxendale." *Texas Wesleyan Law Review* 11 (2004–2005): 249–253.

Gloucester City Council. Gloucester City Council Press Releases. 13 July 2007. http://www.gloucester.gov.uk/YourCouncil/ PressOffice/PressReleases/Archive2007/July2007/ Pressrelease-130707-LegalPlaques.aspx (accessed 28 June 2009).

———. Living Gloucester. http://www.livinggloucester.co.uk/timeline/ 1700s_1900s (accessed 30 June 2009).

Herbert, N. M. "Gloucester: Quay and Docks." British History Online. 1988. http://www.british-history.ac.uk/report.aspx? compid=42306 (accessed 18 July 2009).

Heuston, R. F. V. "James Shaw Willes Tribute." *Northern Ireland Legal Quarterly* 16.2 (1965): 193–215.

Kidwell, John. "Extending the Lessons of Hadley v. Baxendale." *Texas Wesleyan Law Review* 11 (2004–2005): 421–430.

McCamus, John D. *The Law of Contracts.* Toronto: Irwin Law, 2005.

Smiles, Samuel. *Thrift.* Whitefish, MT: Kessinger Publishing Company, 2007.

Chapter 9

Baker, Liva. *Miranda: Crime, Law and Politics.* New York: Atheneum, 1983.

Caldwell, H. Mitchell and Michael Lief. "You Have The Right To Remain Silent: The Strange Story Behind the Most Cited Case in American History." AmericanHeritage.com. http://www .americanheritage.com/articles/magazine/ah/2006/4/2006_4 _48.shtml (accessed 21 August 2009).

Howard Jr., Roscoe C. and Lisa A. Rich. "A History of Miranda and Why It Remains Vital Today." *Valparaiso University Law Review* 40, 2006.

Leo, Richard A. and George C. Thomas, eds. *The Miranda Debate: Law, Justice, and Policing.* Boston: Northeastern University Press, 1998.

Milner, Neak A. *The Court and Local Law Enforcement: The Impact of Miranda.* Beverly Hills, California: Sage Publications, Inc., 1971.

"Miranda v. Arizona." http://en.wikipedia.org/w/index.php?title= Miranda_v._Arizona&oldid=307879202 (accessed 14 August 2009).

Weaver, Russell L. "Miranda at Forty." *San Diego Law Review* 44, 2007.

Weisselberg, Charles D. "Mourning Miranda." *California Law Review* 96.6 (Dec 2008): 1519–1601.

Stuart, Gary L. *Miranda: The Story of America's Right to Remain Silent*. Tucson, AZ: University of Arizona Press, 2008.

Chapter 10

Cosgrove, Richard. *Our Lady the Common Law: An Anglo-American Legal Community 1870–1930*. New York: New York University Press, 1987.

Holmes, Oliver Wendell, Jr. *The Common Law*. Boston: Little, Brown, and Company, 1881.

Holmes, Oliver Wendell, Jr. *Collected Legal Papers*, 270. Gloucester, MA: Peter Smith Publishers, Inc., 1990.

Keats, John. *Endymion*. 1818.

Omychund v. Barker (1744), 26 Eng. Rep. 15.

Index

Index

Index

Index

Index

Inman, Charles, 170

Jack The Ripper, 191
Jackson, Justice Robert H., 205
James, Sir Henry, 25
James Cook University, 146, 147,
 164
Jameson, Lois Ann, 192–196, 198,
 210–212
 assault of, 192–193, 196
Jarndyce v. Jarndyce, 104
Jefferson, President Thomas, 71
Jehovah's Witnesses, 47–51
 publications of, 47, 49, 57,
 65
Jim Crow laws, 92
Johnson, President Lyndon, 203
Jones, T. Elder, 127
Joyce & Co., 169, 170,
 172
Judaism, 46, 98
judges
 disallowing argument at
 trial, 29
 as ordinary persons, 217
 role in democratic society, 42
judgment style, 10, 59, 90
judicial reasoning
 deterrence as motivating factor
 in, 88
 difference between legal and
 political merits of, 104,
 107–109, 156
 effects of personal factors on,
 137, 182–183

influence of cultural affiliations
 on, 65, 98
policy considerations and, 77,
 100–101, 175–176,
 180–181
tendency toward principled
 decisions, 90
judiciary
 conflicts with the rule of law,
 63–65
 creation vs. application of law,
 42, 89
 limits on authority of, 90, 105
juries, 27
 available discretion in awarding
 damages, 176, 179
 disposition toward high damage
 awards, 173, 179
 as finders of fact, 29–30
 unpredictability of, 176
 verdicts, 29–30, 173–174, 198
jurisdiction, 57, 127, 148
Justinian, 77

Keating, Sir Henry Singer, 174,
 180
Keats, John, 188, 215
Kellock, Justice, 57
Kennedy, Jackie, 71
Kent, Justice James, 77
Keon-Cohen, Bryan, 148
King, Martin Luther, Jr., 111

Labour Party, 131
Land Fund (Australia), 158

Index

Index

Index

Index